CW00919896

Stree

**and **

ISBN 0 904491 65 X

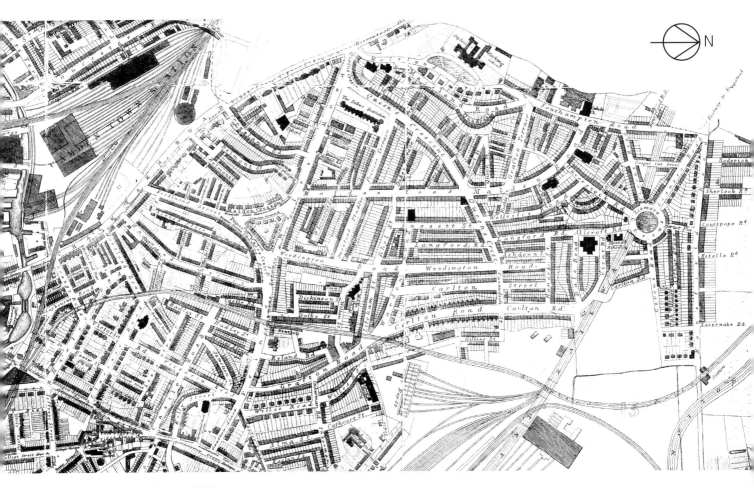

1   Part of St Pancras parish map, 1880

A survey of streets,
buildings & former residents
in a part of Camden

Streets of Gospel Oak
and West Kentish Town

Compiled by Camden History Society

Edited by Steven Denford and David A Hayes

Designed by Ivor Kamlish

General Editor of Camden History Society Publications F Peter Woodford

Diagram of the walks

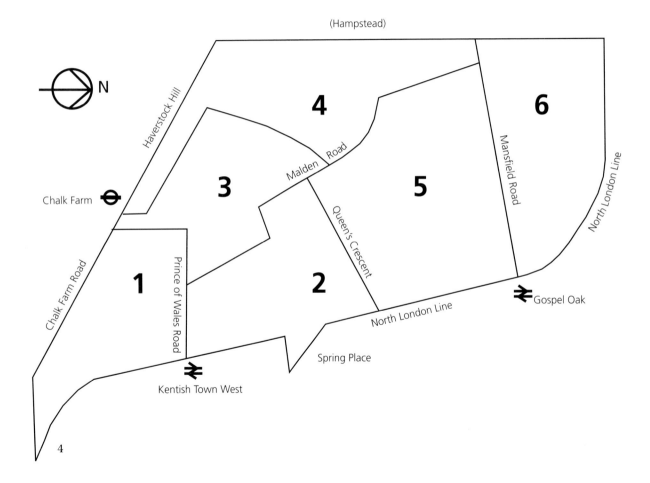

(Hampstead)

N

Haverstock Hill

Chalk Farm

Chalk Farm Road

4

3

Malden Road

Prince of Wales Road

1

Queen's Crescent

2

5

6

Mansfield Road

North London Line

North London Line

Gospel Oak

Spring Place

Kentish Town West

4

Contents

Railways and tramways, with dates of opening

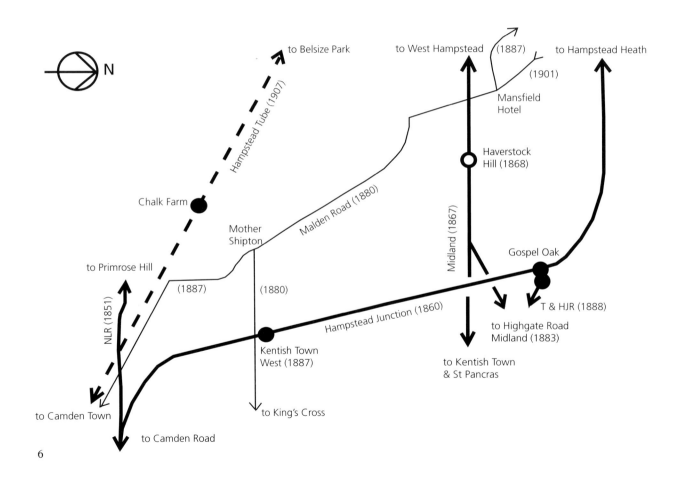

N

to Belsize Park

to West Hampstead

to Hampstead Heath

Hampstead Tube (1907)

(1887)

(1901)

Mansfield Hotel

Haverstock Hill (1868)

Chalk Farm

Mother Shipton

Malden Road (1880)

Midland (1867)

Gospel Oak

to Primrose Hill

(1887)

(1880)

T & HJR (1888)

NLR (1851)

Hampstead Junction (1860)

to Highgate Road Midland (1883)

Kentish Town West (1887)

to Camden Town

to King's Cross

to Kentish Town & St Pancras

to Camden Road

List of illustrations and maps

Historical overview

Kentish Town's historic heart lies to the east of our present survey area, along the old road to Highgate (today's 'High Street'). In our previous volume, *Streets of Kentish Town*, we described the district's evolution from a medieval farming community beside the River Fleet, through a Georgian country town, into a Victorian suburb. Kentish Town was for centuries the main centre of population in St Pancras, a large parish extending south from Highgate to the borders of Holborn and St Giles. Kentish Town's chapel of ease is believed to have dated from the 13th century, and the oldest written reference to the village of 'Kentisston' is in a land transfer deed of 1207.

By contrast, the more westerly neighbourhoods covered in this book are mere youngsters, mostly built up in Victorian times. Until the 1840s, open fields still stretched westward from Kentish Town Road to Haverstock Hill. 'Haverstock' may be identical with the 'Foxhangra' mentioned in 10th-century records of the neighbouring parish of Hampstead. Some suggest that the Haverstock name derived from the Old English for 'place of oats', while others propose the Latin *averia* (for 'pasture') as the root. Only in 1876 was the main road to Hampstead officially numbered throughout as Haverstock Hill, having previously been known simply as either Hampstead Hill or 'the London Road'. The Haverstock name had long been applied to the whole of the area surrounding the road, including much of our survey area.

Within this there were two natural features of note, about which few hard facts survive. The Gospel Oak tree stood near the Hampstead parish boundary but had disappeared by 1821; it had, according to tradition, been a popular venue for outdoor preaching. The Gospel Oak Fields around it continued to be used for an equally ill-documented annual Easter Fair. Through them flowed the Hampstead branch of the River Fleet. Early maps omitted to mark it, but we may deduce from the occasional meandering field boundary that its natural course may have run just east of the present Malden Road. The stream would have met the more easterly Highgate branch at what became Hawley Road, and the river then continued south towards its confluence with the Thames at Blackfriars. By 1814, however, Newton's Hampstead map shows the Hampstead branch running east from near the Gospel Oak, towards a premature junction with the Highgate branch east of Spring Place (p 48). The reasons for this diversion, along what became known locally as the 'Fleet Ditch', are unclear.

Western Kentish Town lay wholly in the manor of Tottenhall, much of which was until 1840 the property of Lord Southampton (see p 11); he leased his fields to local farmers. Some parts of the manor had already been sold to others. By 1761, Dr James Hawley of Leybourne Grange (Kent) had acquired land located at the southern end of our area and extending south into what later became Camden Town. His son, Sir Henry Hawley, went into partnership with Lewis William Buck MP, of Hartland Abbey (Devon) and together they laid out part of the property in 1815 as picturesque gardens. Farther north, the Gospel Oak fields had been bought in 1806 by an Irish peer, Viscount Lismore; while beyond them and bordering Hampstead Heath was land held by the Earls of Mansfield, residents of Kenwood. Three local fields were owned by the Church Lands charity, first recorded in the 16th century, whose revenues helped maintain both the ancient St Pancras parish church (in Pancras Road) and the local Kentish Town chapel-of-ease.

Dairy farming, supplying milk to Londoners, was the main occupation until the later 18th century, when it partly gave way to haymaking, producing fodder for the capital's countless working horses. Some fields became orchards or nursery gardens. As the metropolis continued to expand, others were used for brickmaking.

By late-Georgian times, agriculture was already losing out to house building: dwellings for London's mushrooming population were now seen as a more profitable 'crop'. The 1810s and 1820s saw some early ribbon development along the Hampstead road. In 1835 Lewis William Buck and his son George Stucley Buck together with Sir Joseph Hawley decided to lease their land for building. A great spur to further development was Lord Southampton's decision in 1840 to auction off, in small lots, a large part of his freehold property in West Kentish Town. Some early buyers were charities: the Tailors' Benevolent Institution built its almshouses in Queen's Crescent, while the Orphan Working School occupied the area to the west that became Maitland Park. Most plots, however, were acquired for speculative house building.

Plans drawn up at the time of the Southampton sale had envisaged a network of wide roads, spaciously laid out and lined by detached or semi-detached villas with generous gardens. But the small plots on offer were purchased by numerous small-scale developers of limited means. Although the main roads were laid out very much as intended, the housing built was almost invariably terraced, often without front gardens and with only small back yards. Further streets and mews were squeezed in between the originally proposed roads. A dense street pattern was the result, and until the post-WWII creation of Talacre Open Space, there was no substantial green lung anywhere in West Kentish Town.

The development of our area progressed, very broadly from south to north, mostly between the late 1830s and the early 1870s, apart from Lord Mansfield's northerly estate, completed only in the 1890s. House building was protracted and fitful: the 1860 parish map shows a patchwork of developed sites and of plots yet to be built upon. For decades the district was like one vast building site. Residents felt isolated; other than the occasional horse-bus, transport was poor.

Meanwhile, railways had invaded the area ([1], p 6). The London & Birmingham arrived at Chalk Farm in 1837, followed 14 years later by the North London, its offshoot, whose viaduct marched boldly along our southern boundary. Similarly elevated was the Hampstead Junction line, opened in 1860 along our eastern border. When a few years later the Midland Railway cut its London extension through the Gospel Oak fields, it ran less obtrusively in a cutting, but the upheaval involved in its construction was enormous.

Like the Regent's Canal before them (completed on our southern boundary in 1820), the railways encouraged the northward spread of industry. Sometimes cheek by jowl with the houses of West Kentish Town were small factories serving light industries of many kinds. Pre-eminent among local industries was the making of pianos and their components. Kentish Town (like neighbouring Camden Town) was a world-famous centre of piano manufacture in the days when every self-respecting family aspired to own one.

Most of our area was working-class. Many inhabitants were in 'respectable', skilled occupations such as piano making, or railwaymen with steady, if low-paid, jobs. Though there were a few pockets of real poverty, "mixed" was Charles Booth's description of many local streets when he walked them in 1898 with Police Inspector Tomkin, gathering data for a revision of his well-known poverty maps.

Some middle-class preserves existed on our area's northern and western fringes, where sizeable houses served as the family homes of professionals and businessmen. Interspersed among them was a considerable number of privately-run academies for boys or girls. By the end of the 19th century such properties had often been converted into apartments, and multiple occupation was the norm. 'Haverstock Hill' was the postal address initially assigned to the more westerly streets, lending them a touch of 'Hampstead' respectability. The more easterly reaches of our area were for a while known as 'Kentish New Town' (not to be confused with 'New Kentish Town', which was east of the 'High Street').

Numerous shops of every kind lined the major thoroughfares, while few back streets were without the obligatory corner shop. By 1870 a busy street market had been established in Queen's Crescent, and a second local shopping centre once thrived at Lismore Circus to the north.

Like any Victorian suburb, Gospel Oak and West Kentish Town enjoyed the services of many institutions. A pioneering Board School, opened on Haverstock Hill in 1874, was followed by several others as the child population grew; two of their buildings remain in use as primary schools today. Inhabitants' spiritual needs were met by churches, chapels and mission halls of all denominations (or none). As the population of St Pancras mushroomed in the 19th century, numerous new Anglican 'district' churches were established, each in due course achieving parochial status. Five new parishes lay wholly or partly within our area, three of them dating from the incumbency of Canon Thomas Dale [2]. An energetic proponent of 'Church Extension', this popular vicar of St Pancras (from 1846-60) was commemorated in the naming of a local road.

Transport links improved in 1880 when the London Street Tramways Company laid its tracks along Prince of Wales Road, and up Malden Road to the Mansfield Hotel [1]. Extensions seven years later included a new route towards the West End via Camden Town.

By the 20th century, the housing stock was neglected and overcrowded. Such

2   Rev. Thomas Dale, 'late vicar of St Pancras, Middlesex' (engraved by D J Pound from a photograph by Mayall).

conditions, together with the depredations of two World Wars, led to a major transformation of the area later in the century. Slum clearance, begun between the wars in a limited way, was followed after WWII by redevelopment on a grander scale (see p 12). Started by St Pancras Council in the early 1960s, the project was completed by Camden Council, its successor from 1965. Following the 'comprehensive redevelopment' principles then in vogue with planners, whole streets were swept away. Those surviving were truncated or diverted, so that the earlier street pattern

is now often hard to discern.

In post-WWII West Kentish Town, institutions that had underpinned the community were in decline. With churchgoing less popular, one parish church (St Andrew's) was closed and then demolished in 1953; other parishes have since been combined. In the redeveloped area, new institutions emerged. The 1970s saw a burgeoning of innovative community projects, promoted by local activists, often aided by the Inter-Action charity, which established its first headquarters in West Kentish Town. Its pioneering schemes attracted international interest, and the City Farm it helped to found is still flourishing today.

Gone now are most of the small, 'useful' shops that still traded only a few decades ago, and many of the area's numerous pubs have closed. The street market still functions, though some stall holders are said to be struggling. Some of the Victorian houses that survived the comprehensive redevelopment were rehabilitated as social housing. Others have been 'gentrified' to serve as middle-class family homes, in a return to their original purpose. If now blander and less vibrant than in times past, the area is now more cosmopolitan, and remains just as mixed as it was at the time of Booth's visitation over a century ago.

The Southampton connection

Many of the street names in this book are derived from the original owners of the underlying land. Most of it came from the estate of the 3rd Baron Southampton. This lord was a Fitzroy, descended from Charles II and Barbara Villiers (1641?-1709), created Duchess of Cleveland. In 1670 Charles acknowledged her progeny as Fitzroys and ennobled his first son Charles as Earl (subsequently Duke) of Southampton, a title which died out in 1774.

The second son, Henry, was initially excluded from the peerage, but then Charles changed his mind. He contracted Henry in marriage to 5-year-old Isabella, heiress of Henry Bennet, Earl of Arlington; sixteen days later Henry was made Earl of Euston (the Arlingtons' estate in Suffolk) and was named in the patent as Henry Fitzroy. Isabella brought the copyhold of the manor of Tottenhall in North London to the eventual marriage in 1679. Three years later the King created Henry the 1st Duke of Grafton, and he continued in royal favour when James II came to the throne. Henry died in 1690 from the musket wound he received when he led the assault on Passage Way during the Churchill campaign in Ireland.

His son, Charles Henry (1683-1757) became the 2nd Duke. He wisely obtained from the owners of Tottenhall Manor, the Canons of St Paul's Cathedral, a fresh lease of '3 lives' in 1723, shortly after the death of his mother Isabella who had held the reversionary interest in the manor from the Crown. He was succeeded by his grandson Augustus Henry (1735-1811), while his younger grandson Charles inherited the interest in Tottenhall Manor. (Their father had died in 1741.)

Charles Fitzroy became a soldier, a politician, and a prominent courtier. He married Anne Warren, the daughter and co-heiress of Admiral Sir Peter Warren and had no fewer than 16 children. The family lived at Fitzroy Farm, which stood in about 100 acres of demesne land at the north end of Tottenhall Manor, east of Kenwood in Highgate. The estate was landscaped "with much taste" by fashionable landscape designers, including Capability Brown and Humphrey Repton.

Charles was a political agent for his brother, the 3rd Duke, for instance acting as intermediary in the negotiations with William Pitt the Elder when Grafton was taking over as Prime Minister from Pitt. In 1768 Grafton as PM ensured the passage of an Act of Parliament vesting "the freehold of the Manor of Tottenhall in Charles Fitzroy, brother of Augustus Henry, 3rd Duke of Grafton", subject to payment of ground rent of £300 per annum to the previous freeholders, the Canons of St Paul's Cathedral. Already by 1837, before much building had taken place, the legality of this Act was being questioned. An article in the *Morning Chronicle* estimated that by then the family had paid £18,000 to St Paul's but had received £1.5 million income from the land.

Within a few years Charles Fitzroy fell out with his brother and went his own way. He remained in government in 1775, refusing to follow his brother's disapproval of Lord North's American policies. He was rewarded in 1780 when he was created Baron Southampton of Southampton. He died in 1797 and was buried in St James' burial ground in Hampstead Road.

In 1806 his son and heir the 2nd Baron Southampton (1761-1810), George Ferdinand sold the two Gospel Oak Fields to Cornelius O'Callaghan, 1st Viscount Lismore (1775-1857), an Irish peer, who later auctioned them for building land when he was ordered to do so in 1846 by the Court of Chancery.

Parts of the Tottenham Manor were also sold off by the 2nd Baron during the early 19th century, apparently to pay for gambling debts. In August 1840, George Ferdinand's son Charles, 3rd Baron Southampton (1804-1872) ([**3**], p 12) auctioned off for building nearly all that was left of the estate in a sale that lasted 3 days. A smaller sale followed in 1841, which ended the family's connection with the Manor of Tottenhall.

3 Charles Fitzroy, 3rd Baron Southampton (by R Ackermann, *New Sporting Magazine*, 1836)

Local redevelopment

Few houses in Gospel Oak and West Kentish Town were well built, and its social status was sealed after it was encircled by railways. By the turn of the 20th century overcrowding was rife. In 1921 it was estimated that 11,000 people in St Pancras lived 3 to a room, many of them in our survey area. There were high levels of unemployment; by 1922 10,000 people in the borough were out of work. The local piano industry was in decline, unable to compete with German and American products. Meanwhile, the houses in Gospel Oak were crumbling. A survey of the Church Lands estates in 1939 suggested that leaseholders were willing to do outstanding repairs, but the outbreak of war frustrated their intentions. The removal of front railings for war munitions was a final discouragement.

The borough of St Pancras had started a house-building programme in 1904 and by 1939 it had succeeded in completing its 1000th flat. Meanwhile the St Pancras House Improvement Society, later the St Pancras Housing Association, was tackling the real poverty of Litcham Street, by replacing the overcrowded properties

there with the modern flats of the Athlone Estate, which first opened in 1933. Despite these efforts it was estimated in 1939 that 3,000 people were still living in seriously overcrowded conditions, exacerbated by destruction caused by war-time bombing.

As the war in Europe neared its end, St Pancras Council decided at its meeting on 2 May 1945 to use the limited materials and labour available to provide as many housing units as possible from the existing housing stock before embarking on large-scale new schemes. In the meantime, land would be purchased for future estates and surveys carried out in areas of severe deprivation. One such survey had already been made by the Medical Officer of Health, in the Queen's Crescent area. By 1949, there was talk of the Council rebuilding half the borough within the next 20 years. Good progress was being made elsewhere, but little was seen in Gospel Oak until 1951, when work was started on Powell and Moya's Barrington Court by Lamble Street. This development and the later Kiln Place stand on the site of old brickworks, where there were fewer problems of ownership to be solved than in areas with existing housing, where compulsory powers had to be used. Until 1965, the planning of such areas needed the agreement of both the London County Council, as overall planning authority, and the Ministry of Housing and Local Government. In 1951 the Ministry refused redevelopment permission for a part of Allcroft Road "in view of the large number of occupied houses and the small increase in accommodation which would result if the land was cleared and new dwellings erected". This bureaucratic hiccup was soon overcome, but the reasoning was to be remembered 15 years later in Oak Village.

The 1950s and early 1960s were heady days in planning and architectural circles. Gospel Oak and West Kentish Town (Housing Area No.2) was seen by some as the most likely part of the borough for total redevelopment. A proposal was sent to the LCC in October 1962 for the whole district from Hampstead Heath to Chalk Farm to be designated a Comprehensive Redevelopment Area. Visions of Corbusian *Unités d'Habitations* set amidst parkland, marching down from Savernake Road to Chalk Farm, suddenly seemed within reach. However, this application fell flat not least because the vast area was neither a level playing field nor a levelled one: redevelopment of individual parts of the district was already steadily continuing, and this had compromised the grand design.

Demolition of streets in Gospel Oak began in 1963 **[4]**, but other influences were soon brought to bear. In 1965 the Leasehold Reform Act transformed the Church Lands estates by giving their longstanding tenants the right to buy their freeholds. Housing associations were also beginning to offer attractive alternatives of partial home ownership. In some comprehensive redevelopment areas new owner-occupiers were buying into the existing housing stock, sometimes with the help of council improvement grants. And however well designed the new Estates might be, there was a growing feeling that a completely municipalised Kentish Town might not be so attractive without a few markers from the past for the local community. Tom Dixon, the vicar of St Martin's Church during the redevelopment of Gospel Oak, has written about this in his book *Operation Skyscraper*.

Evidence that the planners, too, recognised the needs of people within the new environments comes from the West Kentish Town Planning Consultants' Report No.3 of 1964. Messrs Armstrong and MacManus were the architects for the main Gospel Oak scheme and their team included Gordon Cullen, Kenneth Brown and Ian Nairn, whose ideas on 'townscape' carried considerable weight at the time. Their brief was to suggest how the new Estates in West Kentish Town (to the south of Queen's Crescent) might be better integrated with the existing buildings and streets that were to remain. Although they begin with the remark "there is not much that is really worth preserving", they continue with an astute analysis of the new and the old. "The new dwellings are 5 and 6 storeys high so that most people live off the ground. This allows wider spacing and gives proper daylight and open space. But inevitably, the street disappears and the ground belongs to everybody and nobody." By contrast, the old layout, for all its monotony, was of human scale. "The streets created a sense of progression, of life, as they led the eye from one place to the next, or revealed fresh vistas. The ground was personal to the people and not anonymous." Nevertheless, the redevelopment of West Kentish Town and Gospel Oak proceeded apace.

At the end of 1965 houses in Elaine Grove and Julia Street were included in the compulsory purchase order (CPO) for Phases 7, 8 and 9. A public meeting was held in March 1966. The Chair of Planning of the recently formed Camden Borough Council, Peggy Duff, insisted that planning officers should be exposed to the views of the public. Phase 9 was the final phase of the scheme and also included Oak Village, for which a CPO had not yet been made. In Oak Village there were 20 owner-occupiers who had restored their cottages with the help of Council improvement grants, and another 18 similar properties had been improved by developers before being sold. It was revealed that if the cottages were to remain there would be no loss of housing units in Phase 9. So why pull them down?

The resolution to include the Oak Village properties in the CPO came before the Council on 21 December 1966. Amid considerable political embarrassment,

4 Haverstock Road before demolition,
with the new Bacton High Rise (p 89) ahead
(photo Michael Ogden)

an opposition amendment to scrap the
proposal was carried, and the proposal
was withdrawn. On 15 February 1967,
Oak Village was officially removed from
the CPO, as were most of the properties
in Julia Street and Elaine Grove later in
the year. Finally, in 1968 the Minister of
Housing refused to confirm the CPO on
the remaining tenanted houses.

It was a famous victory, and not just for
the inhabitants. The demolition of Oak
Village was indefensible in planning terms,
and should never have been sought. In
future, more care would be needed on the
part of planners in listening to the voices
of self-interest, both private and public,
and above all, the voices of reason. Phase
9 of the Gospel Oak Redevelopment was
finally completed, in its reduced form, in
1981. The physical framework for another
century was in place.

But the task continues of turning that
framework into a community where
everyone is prepared to share and
contribute to making it liveable. It will
need continual financial support and local
commitment if, this time round, the vision
of all its designers is to be realised.

Present street names and their origins

Allcroft
John Derby, glovemaker and
financier of St Martin's Church

Arctic
Former Franklin Street
renamed by association
with arctic explorer Sir
John Franklin (1786-1847)

Ashdown
Edwin*, of Malden Crescent

Athlone
Princess Alice, Countess of,
opened Athlone House flats

Baptist
St John the Baptist
(variant on earlier St John's)

Barrington
Somerset village †

Bassett
George, brickfield owner and
agent to Lord Southampton

Belmont
Street built over the grounds
of Belmont House

Castle
Former Kentish Town inn

Castlehaven
Elizabeth, Countess of,
buried in St Pancras Churchyard †

Chalk Farm
Farmhouse near Primrose
Hill, once called Chalcots

Clarence
William, Duke of, later William IV †

Coity
Coalmine at Blaenavon †
(cf. Talacre and see p 42)

Collard
& Collard, piano makers

Courthope
MBW naming, unexplained

Craddock
William, bootmaker*

Cressfield
Watercress grew locally

Crogsland
Old English *crog* (crooked)?

Dalby
Jasper Boniston Dalby*,
house proprietor?

Dale
Rev. Thomas, C19
vicar of St Pancras

Dunboyne
Remote Fitzroy family*
connection (see p 77)?

Elaine
Heroine in Arthurian legend?
(street formerly Arthur Grove)

Estelle
MBW naming, unexplained

Ferdinand
George Ferdinand Fitzroy,
2nd Baron Southampton*

Forge
Old forge or smithy on site

Gilden
Gilden Road once lay nearby

15

Gillies
Margaret (1803-87), painter
and Kentish Town resident

Grafton
Duke of, head of Fitzroy family★,
lords of Tottenhall manor

Harmood
Henry and Mary★,
Tottenhall tenants c.1800

Hartland
Abbey, North Devon
property of Buck family★

Haven
Contraction of Castlehaven

Haverstock
Latin *averia* (pasture) or
Old English for 'place of oats'?

Hawley
Sir Joseph★, co-developer
of Hawley-Buck estate

Hemingway
Ernest, American novelist,
safarist in East Africa (cf. Meru)

Herbert
Vincent, a Hoxton builder★

Julia
Relation of John
Furnell★, builder?

Kiln
On site of kiln yard of
Gospel Oak Brick Works

Kingsford
Unexplained

Lamble
Samuel, master builder &
St Pancras Vestryman★

Leybourne
Kent seat of Hawley family★

Lismore
Cornelius O'Callaghan, Viscount★,
bought Gospel Oak Fields in 1806

Maitland
Family, C18-C19 benefactors
of Orphan Working School

Malden
Surrey parish, location of
a Fitzroy family★ estate

Mansfield
Earl of, Kenwood resident★

Marsden
Thomas, wholesale druggist★

Meru
Tanzanian mountain (reflecting
occupation by African refugees)

Modbury
South Devon village from which
Ponsford family★ hailed

Mutton
Shoulder of Mutton Field

Newbury
Variant on Newberry; Thomas
Weeding★ married Elizabeth
Newberry

Oak
The Gospel Oak tree

Powlett
Unexplained

Prince of Wales
Albert Edward, future Edward VII †

Quadrant
Surrounding roads
describe a quarter circle

Queen's
Queen Victoria †

Rhyl
North Wales resort †
(cf. Prince of *Wales*)

(New) Rochford
Essex town? †

Roderick
MBW naming, unexplained

Rona
MBW naming, unexplained

St Ann's
An unidentified 'Ann'
(related to the builder),
with added 'Saint' prefix?

St Leonard's
Unexplained

St Silas
Early Christian martyr
(eponymous church adjoins)

St Thomas'
Analogous to St Ann's (q.v.)?

Savernake
Forest 10 miles from
Wiltshire home village
of William Turner★

Shirlock
MBW naming, unexplained

Southampton
Charles Fitzroy, 3rd Baron★

Spring
Water source feeding River Fleet

Talacre
Flintshire coalmining
village near Rhyl (q.v.) †

Thurlow
Rev. Edward & Rev. Charles★

Truro
Origin unknown

Vicars
Rev. Thomas Dale, C19
vicar of St Pancras

Warden
(Church) warden?

Weedington
Thomas Weeding, City merchant
& St Pancras churchwarden★

Wellesley
Arthur, Duke of Wellington (d.1852) †

Wilkin
Miss Mary Jacomb Wilkin,
private school directress★

Woodyard
Yard of timber merchant
Bignell George Elliot

Pancras Vale

Circular walk from Chalk Farm station
For modern map see back cover

Pancras Vale was the name given in the early 19th century to the stretch of the highway to Hampstead between the Regent's Canal and Haverstock Hill that began to be built up with houses during the Regency. For a time the name was also applied to the district that was developed to the east. Only 15 houses on the west side of the road (outside our survey area) were numbered as part of Pancras Vale; the houses on the east side were either individually named or formed terraces. In 1863 the street, by now fully built up, was renamed Chalk Farm Road from its proximity to the ancient Chalk Farm. The district to the east was sometimes also called Chalk Farm, although it is now generally considered part of Kentish Town.

The first side road off Pancras Vale was built in the 1820s and another was begun in the next decade but most of the area of our walk dates from the 1840s. Some of the original houses survive, although the street layout has been altered after bombing in WWII followed by comprehensive redevelopment plans (luckily only partially carried out).

The area of our walk was literally a green field site until the 19th century, as can be seen from the 1804 Thompson map, which shows no buildings on the 3 fields delineated. From north to south these were Washey Ten Acres and Shoulder of Mutton Field, both farmed by Richard Morgan of Kentish Town; and south towards the then site of the parish workhouse (now Camden Town Underground station) the Seven Acre Field (in fact 18 acres in extent) farmed by Mr Leslie of Pleasant Row, Camden Town. The three fields corresponded to the three underlying estates – Southampton, Harmood and Hawley-Buck.

Turning left out of Chalk Farm Underground station, cross over Adelaide Road by the traffic lights and continue across Regent's Park Road, by the side of a tall wall and an old drinking fountain, and with a view of the Roundhouse ahead. Walking south, stay on this side of the main road (described in *Streets of Camden Town*) for a better view of the buildings opposite. **CHALK FARM ROAD** begins at the junction with Crogsland Road (p 55). In 1885 it was renumbered from No.36 upwards so that the first house opposite, then No.82, became No.89. Before 1863 the varied houses on this stretch of road as far as the next turning (Ferdinand Street) had been known as Caroline Place. Begun in 1812 these were the first buildings on this part of the Southampton estate, auctioned in 1840 in lots for further building development. By then the railway – in the shape of the London & Birmingham's huge goods yard and Chalk Farm station (no trace of which survives) – had arrived opposite, and the middle-class, residential nature of the houses changed, with many converted or extended into commercial premises.

The present **No.89**, the tall building on the corner, is now a hotel. It retains some of its 19th-century façade, although it was gutted inside when it was converted in 1975 from Nos.88&89 into a Turkish restaurant. This became the Kypriana Hotel in 1981, and more recently, the Camden Lock Hotel. It lies on the site of No.23 Caroline Place, home to James Pearson (d.1866) who ran the Eschol Nursery (p 55) on the land behind. After his death, the auctioneer, estate agent and tax collector George Smith was based here until the early 20th century. Next to the hotel, behind a café, is an original, stuccoed 2-storey building, **No.87**, which stretches back to an old bakehouse behind, remaining from the time in the mid-19th century when John and Mary Miller ran a baker's and confectioner's here, as well as a post office. The bakehouse is clearly visible because the adjoining site of Nos.81-86 is now taken up by a petrol station, here since 1961. One of the first buildings on this site was detached Chace (later Chase) Cottage, named after Joseph Chace who had leased the land on which to build the property in 1814. In 1871 the Russian-born photographer James Monte was living there; he operated twelve different photographic and artistic studios throughout north London during the years 1862-1890, including one at Alexandra Palace. James opened his last studio in 1891 at Southend-on-Sea, where he retired. His three sons – James, George and Richard, the first two born in the house – all became professional photographers and were important in the early development of the cinema in the UK, each becoming travelling showmen, demonstrating film clips at fairs in the years before WWI. Also making way for the filling station was former Rochelle Cottage (No.20 Caroline Place), where the piano maker George Nutting, in business since the 1820s, was living in the 1850s and 1860s.

Continue to the side wall of **No.80**, which once supported an arched entrance to the Peniel Tabernacle, a Baptist chapel that was opened on land behind the then No.74 Chalk Farm Road in late 1866. It could seat 600 people. When it closed, the chapel was bought at auction in 1881 by the Salvation Army, which founded here its Chalk Farm Citadel. Its early meetings were often disrupted by "roughs" gathering outside, angered no doubt by the Army's stance on alcohol and entertainment. In 1882 the Chalk Farm Salvation Army band was founded – one of the oldest, it was world famous, and is still a familiar sight

and sound in the local streets. At the very youthful age of 18, Alfred W Punchard was appointed its bandmaster in 1894, an association which was to continue until his death in 1950. He held the position of Corps Bandmaster, and latterly that of National Bandmaster, for fifty years. The Citadel was moved in 1923 to nearby No.10 Haverstock Hill (p 68), but the Salvation Army retained the hall until 1958 when its site was cleared, subsequently to become part of the petrol station.

The 2-storey buildings Nos.78-80 beyond the garage date from 1865 after a new side turning, Belmont Street (p 38), had been formed. They cover the site of Nos.16 and 17 Caroline Place. In 1848 a small brewery was opened here by Mr Hanbury, Ralph Jackson and Charles Barclay, alongside a new dairy run by Miss Charlotte Arthur. In 1862 she moved to No.21 (later No.86 Chalk Farm Road), continuing in business until the end of the century. In the same year the brewery was purchased by a Mr Vandergasteele. That is how the rate books show him; in local directories he is listed as Lewis Castile. He more likely to have been Louis Vandecasteele, born in 1815 in Eernegem, Belgium, where there used to be a Vandecasteele brewery. He called his property the Bavarian Brewery. Unfortunately, its records do not appear to have survived, but if, as the name suggests, it was brewing German-style lager in the

early 1860s this would make it the earliest brewery to do so in the UK. In 1865 the brewery was mortgaged to Francis Edward Tucker who renamed it the Chalk Farm Brewery, spending considerable sums in enlarging it and rebuilding the properties along the main road: the shop at No.80 and the brewery tap on the corner (Nos.78&79). The outlay bankrupted him, and Vandecasteele repossessed the brewery and sold it and its contents at auction in September 1866. The brewery tap on the corner continued as a pub known for well over a century (until 1991) as the Belmont Tavern. In the 1880s it had a large concert hall attached to it. After a spell as the Engine Room, the pub has now become **Bartok**, advertised as London's only classical music bar.

On the opposite corner of Belmont Street is a modern block at **Nos.74-77**. It is called The Chalk House. On its site were two early villas (Nos.12 and 13&14 Caroline Place), later built out at ground floor level to form shops. At No.76 (then No.69) Domenico Gatti, a member of the famous family of Ticinese restaurateurs, ran refreshment rooms from 1864 to 1876. The shops and villas were demolished in 1964 to make way for a car showroom. This changed hands a number of times before the present building was constructed on the site in 2003. It houses a Sainsbury's local and an Italian restaurant, and expensive private apartments above.

Beyond are **Nos.72-73**, Belgo Noord, a restaurant specialising in Belgian food and beer, which opened here in April 1992. The architect was Ron Arad, who also designed the opera house in Tel Aviv, where he was born in 1951. No.72 was earlier the first base of Inter-Action (p 54). Belgo Noord is attached to a 3-bay property once known as Belmont House (at No.11 Caroline Place), which had stabling for six horses and carriages. The house was built by George Murray, who had leased the land for building in 1817 and who was still living here in 1841. There were extensive grounds behind, upon which were built the two arms of Belmont Street (p 38), which we visit at the end of this walk.

There follows a late-19th-century 3-storey terrace, **Nos.67-70**. Clearly visible on the side wall of No.67 is a painted advert for Bacon & Sons, Stationers. Bacon's Library, a bookseller and stationer's business which doubled as a post office, was at No.63 (renumbered No.70) from the 1860s until the early 20th century. In common with other post offices during the Victorian period it acted as an employment exchange where servants and others advertised for work. For some 30 years from the late 1950s Nos.67-70 formed the base of W R Harvey & Co (Antiques) Ltd until their move to Witney, Oxfordshire. They advertised that their showrooms were in a 300-year-old farmhouse and in 1971 made the bizarre claim that this building was the original Chalk Farm.

The terrace block does, however, front the old Wilfred Cottage, the earliest building in Caroline Place, the building lease having been let in 1812. In 1853, by when it was simply No.10, it housed the North West Gymnasium and School of Arms, run by Ammond (otherwise Eamonn) Winterbottom and offering fencing classes and gymnastics for gentlemen and callisthenics for ladies; this closed 15 years later and Oliver Bacon, the stationer, moved in to the house.

Set back behind the shops at **Nos.65-66** is a once detached villa property, with a projecting central bay, stuccoed and presently painted a rather garish pink. This house was begun as Cumberland Lodge in 1814. After the death of its owner John Madeley, it was sold at auction in 1842, when it had ornamental gardens, a conservatory and hot houses, plus stables entered from Ferdinand Street. By 1857 it had become the Oxford and Cambridge pub, with its own music hall, called the Blenheim. Its large grounds included a racket court and a billiards saloon, which can be seen on the OS map of 1870. In that year, however, the pub closed and was sold; Chappell's piano factory (p 38) was extended over part of its grounds.

The gable end of the old factory can be seen rising above the low building that houses the Majestic Wine Warehouse. Next to its forecourt, amidst a mass of greenery, is the gated entrance to cobbled Old Dairy Mews. This leads past what remains of the villa known as Northville, now **No.62**, to a loft reached by stairs that is the base for the architectural firm Ron Arad Associates, founded in 1989. In the villa's grounds were stables, also reached from Ferdinand Street. By 1900 these had become Dixon's Bottling Works.

Set back from the next run of single-storey shops, more houses of Caroline Place dating from the Regency period can be made out. Behind **Nos.57-58**, now a branch of Nando's restaurant chain, is detached No.6. Next to it is No.5, built as Rose Villa in 1817, which became the coal offices of the London & North Western Railway Company in the mid-19th century. The once pretty No.1 Caroline Place (formerly Grove Cottage) can be seen behind **Nos.50-51**. It abuts a pub built in 1850 on the corner of Ferdinand Street and called the Monarch, which was licensed as a theatre from 1854 to 1863. More recently, the pub became Barfly at The Monarch, but since 2005 has been simply **Barfly**. One of Camden's oldest music venues, it has attracted rock and indie fans for several years; it is suitably scruffy.

Crossing at the zebra to the opposite side of Chalk Farm Road, turn right, past the pub, and cross Ferdinand Street (p 31). On the opposite corner note the West Indian scene painted on the side of the Jamaican restaurant at **No.48**, currently closed. The houses at **Nos.40-48** date from the late 1820s, when they were built as Ferdinand Terrace. They present an intriguing variety of shapes, including some prominent crooked chimney stacks. Since 1990 Nos.40-42 have housed a Wetherspoon's pub, the **Man in the Moon**. In the 1890s No.41 was a clothier's and draper's, a store typical of the Victorian age – there were then half a dozen in Chalk Farm Road. After WWI it housed furniture dealers, which proliferated along the road in the 1930s.

Beyond the pub is the 3-storey 1860s pair of **Nos.38-39** adjoining the very tall and fussily detailed **Nos.36-37**. The latter now houses the pawnbrokers Harvey and Thompson, which at the turn of the millennium took over the old family firm of pawnbrokers and jewellers G W Thomson [sic], long based here and to whom the inscription "Established 1837" relates.

The Victorian buildings replaced former Nos.1-4 Harmood Place, part of a terrace that stretched either side of Harmood Street (p 26) and was erected from 1822 on what was the Harmood estate (p 25). Isaac Gibbs and his son Alexander, artists in stained glass, were based at No.2 in the mid-19th century. Alexander Gibbs designed the central light of the east window in nearby Holy Trinity church. In March 1854 the firm was offering a £2 reward for the safe return of a brown

parcel containing designs.

On the opposite corner of Harmood Street is No.35, known since 1982 as the **Lock Tavern**, from the proximity of Camden Lock and its market. It started life in the early 1820s as the Wellington Arms, but with the coming of the railway in the next decade changed its name to the Railway Tavern. In Chapter 6 of *Dombey and Son*, Dickens describes the havoc that the railway initially wreaked on 'Camberling Town', likening its arrival to an earthquake. Later in the book, Dickens notes that the neighbourhood "which had hesitated to acknowledge the railroad in its straggling days… now boasted of its powerful and prosperous relation. There were railway patterns in its drapers' shops, and railway journals in the windows of its newsmen". Life imitates Art. The Railway Tavern boasted of its fine view of the two huge chimneys in the goods yard, which ventilated the engine powering the continuous cable that, in the railway's first decade, was used to haul trains up the incline from Euston. This was before the great yellow-brick wall opposite was built in about 1854 to enclose and buttress the goods yard. The wall soon became dark and forbidding, blackened with coal dust and soot. Many of the earlier inhabitants of the terraces along Pancras Vale moved out and it became the shopping street it remains to this day. In the 1850s the engraver Edwin Roffe wrote that "Pancras

Vale is more like a valley of dismal dumps than anything else – coal shoots pollute its once fragrant air".

Auctions and inquests were regularly held at the pub in the mid-Victorian period, although it was decided that the inquest into the death of the 64-year-old local surveyor Septimus Hopkins, after an incident at the pub in November 1865, was best held elsewhere. The landlord, Richard Parry, was committed to trial for having severely beaten Hopkins, when the latter tried to re-enter the pub after being ejected. At the subsequent trial, the jury felt Parry had a right to act in this manner although the judge commented it was a shame that a man should lose his life "for such a trumpery cause".

Lock Tavern and the house alongside make up the sole remnant of former Harmood Place. The last building in the terrace, tiny No.8, once stood by the entrance to a large timber yard and factory that stretched to Harmood Grove (p 26). This later became Carter & Paterson's carrier business **[5]**. The site of Nos.7 & 8 Harmood Place is now taken up by the Chalk Farm Service Station, which dates from 1963, three other houses to the corner of Hartland Road having been demolished the year before. These houses (Nos.29-31) had been built in 1847 on the Hawley-Buck estate, which fronted the remainder of Chalk Farm Road. The boundary between this estate and the Harmood estate ran

5 Nos.32&33 Chalk Farm Road, showing Carter & Paterson's carriers' yard (Ernest Milner, 1903)

behind between Harmood Street and Hartland Road, following an old footpath.

Past Hartland Road (p 25) the terraced houses dating from the early 1840s development of the Hawley-Buck estate have all, happily, survived. Nos.20-28 and Nos.10-19, the two terraces either side of Hawley Street ahead, were built as Hampton Terrace. This was developed mainly by the builder George Edward Sewell, who also built much of the area immediately behind. Unlike the earlier houses we have passed to this point, these had no front gardens. They now share the livery of buildings further down the main road by Camden Lock, painted in bright colours and in some cases sporting large and jaunty fibre-glass models (for example, the enormous rocking chair on **No.19**). The shops stock similar items – boots and shoes, fashion and leather goods – while some offer tattoos and body piercing.

No.20 is the shop formerly owned by the artist formerly known as Prince! In front of a vast crowd in 1993, the diminutive pop star opened No.20 as Sign of The Times, painted in his trademark purple and dedicated to selling Prince-related paraphernalia. He was top of the charts at the time, but as his star faded the shop did too, closing in October 1996. It is now painted black and carries a large metal dragonfly, reflecting the current firm's name. **No.14**, once No.5 Hampton Terrace, was a double-fronted shop boasting large plate-glass windows as early as 1848. Later in the century, along with No.13 it housed the Chalk Farm Picture Frame Manufactory, established in 1860. In the 1850s, **No.12** was Snell's the "chymist's" (and also a Post Office), while **No.10** (then No.1 Hampton Terrace) was a butcher's shop run by William Whitlam, whose family business remained here until WWI. Past its door cattle would have been herded on the hoof to Smithfield Market, having been unloaded into cattle pens alongside the Roundhouse from 1848 to 1854. The pens were then relocated to Maiden Lane where the new Caledonian Cattle Market was soon to open.

Cross Castlehaven Road by the traffic lights under the railway bridge and continue along the last section of Chalk Farm Road, making your way through the throng that is normally here, since the main entrance to the Camden Lock market lies opposite. The terrace beyond the railway, called Frances (or Francis) Terrace until 1863, was begun in the early 1840s. The **Caernarvon** (once Carnarvon) **Castle** at Nos.7&8 has, after a brief spell as the Fusilier & Firkin, recently reverted to its original name, now re-spelt with modern English spelling. In the 19th century there was a great influx into Camden Town and its locality of migrants from the Celtic nations (as navvies, dairymen and so on) and it's been said that a separate pub was "provided" for each group – the Dublin Castle and the

Edinboro Castle, both in Camden Town, for the Irish and Scots respectively, and the Carnarvon Castle for the Welsh. In the 1960s the pub was, unusually, host to *both* Mods and Rockers. The last house is **No.1**, built in the early 1850s and now Punky Fish (the shop with the large fibreglass fish adorning its front). On its side wall are the remains of a huge advert which the then shopkeeper Robert Edwards had painted in the 1890s. This is above the entrance to Camden Canal Market, which was then the entrance to the Bignell Elliott sawmills that were based in Hawley Wharf, until WWII. Until his death in 1933 these were owned by Bignell George Elliott, who was made a KBE in 1918 and who was involved in a number of charities.

We have now reached the canal. Pause on the bridge for a view left towards Hawley Lock and the jokey, post-modern design of the former TV-am building. The first bridge over the canal here was built in 1815 but began to collapse under the weight of road traffic before it was replaced in 1876-1877 by a new road bridge; this was criticised for the necessary but conspicuous girder which divided the roadway.

Return to CASTLEHAVEN ROAD and turn right, into the western part of the Hawley-Buck estate, which stretches east to Kentish Town Road. The section of the road as far as the railway line ahead was laid out in 1841 as Grange Road and the buildings that once lined it on both sides

were erected mainly in the mid-1840s. The Hawley family home was Leybourne Grange in Kent. The road was renumbered in 1885 and then renamed in 1938 along with Victoria Road beyond the railway line, with a name chosen at random from a gravestone at Old St Pancras Church, that of Elizabeth, Countess of Castlehaven, buried there in 1743.

Pass the **Hawley Arms**, the first building in the road, dating from 1841; note the authentic family heraldry on its sign. Opposite is the short **LEYBOURNE STREET**, whose name also recalls the Hawley's Kentish seat. The street was developed in 1846 with terraced houses on both sides: Nos.1-5 on the right faced Nos. 6-10, erected by the ubiquitous George Sewell. The old houses were damaged in WWII, and demolished in the mid-1970s. The left-hand side was redeveloped by the Council early in the next decade, facing the large open space it had laid out.

We now cross **HAVEN STREET**, right. Named as such in 1938, as a contraction of Castlehaven, it was developed as Grange Street in the 1840s, when it was lined with 23 houses. None remain. Prominent is the old North London Line viaduct through which access to Camden Canal Market can be obtained. In one of its arches, in the 1860s, a Sunday school attached to Holy Trinity Church, Hartland Road, catered for, on average, 35 poor local children.

A pink brick side wall takes up much

of the east side of the former Grange Street. It belongs to Cameron House at **No.12 Castlehaven Road**, a 2-storey light-industrial unit constructed in the mid-1980s by the Council and housing a number of businesses. It stretches to the corner of the next street on your right.

This is **LEYBOURNE ROAD**. The part of the road beyond the bend, which we shall not explore, was first developed as Exeter Road South, as it led into Exeter Road (now Torbay Street), outside our area. Many of its houses, developed in the mid-1840s, were short-lived, falling victim either to the North London line in the late 1840s or to the Hampstead Junction Railway a decade later. Leybourne Road itself once stretched across Castlehaven Road to meet up with Hawley Road beyond the open space to our left; the houses along it there were heavily bombed in WWII. In 1898 Charles Booth walked this area accompanied by the local police Inspector W Tomkin to update his poverty map. He described Leybourne Road as "very rough…with some thieves". The present road is now entirely commercial in character, its railway arches mostly used by car repair firms.

Now carefully cross over Castlehaven Road (busy one-way traffic from your left) to the pathway opposite. To your right the railway viaduct obliterated No.15 Grange Road, which from September 1851 to January 1854 housed the Camden

Town branch of the Mormon Church, at a time when it was encouraging converts to emigrate to Salt Lake City.

The path follows the former line of Leybourne Road. To our right a playground was laid out after WWII before the present open space was redeveloped. The path passes the centre of the **Castlehaven Community Association** at No.33 Hawley Road, here since 1987. It runs a summer playscheme and IT classes for elderly people. The Hopeful Monsters Under 5s group is also based here. (At the time of writing the path was temporarily closed; if it still is, continue under the railway bridge and take the first turning left and pass under another railway bridge to reach the front of the Association's building.)

Beyond the centre, pause when we reach the junction of Hawley Road and **HAWLEY STREET**, stretching away to our left. Both were named after the ground landlords. Before 1886 Hawley Street was known as Hawley Road West. The former houses along its southern side were developed by the Marylebone Building Society in the mid-1840s, while those facing them, built slightly later by George Sewell, were called Hawley Road Villas until 1873. No.2 Hawley Villas was home in 1848 to the painter H Lancaster who exhibited at the Royal Society of British Artists. Just short of the junction with the main road (then Pancras Vale) a

turning on the northern side led to Hawley Mews; again built by Sewell, in 1847, this comprised 18 coach houses and 3-stall stables, with carmen living in the rooms above.

The Council's scheme for the demolition of the dwellings in Hawley Street and Hawley Mews was approved in 1976 but put on hold for several years for lack of funding. In 1984 a group of squatters in Hawley Mews occupied an old glass factory, naming it The Glasshouse, in which they planned to provide music and a community centre. Their scheme was short-lived because demolition of all the buildings in Hawley Mews began soon afterwards; the mews is now just a service road behind the late-1980s flats at **Nos.1-39**.

On the corner of Hawley Street and Hawley Road, the large building opposite was built in 1849 as a pub, the Stag's Head. It has recently been converted into private flats known as **Stag Apartments**, with a glazed roof-top storey added. Cross over to it and continue along the north-western end of **HAWLEY ROAD**. This was begun in the late 1830s as a turning out of Kentish Town Road (to the east, outside our area). The houses in this stretch were developed in the 1840s, and were renumbered in 1858, after construction of the railway viaduct of the Hampstead Junction Railway had begun. This obliterated former No.23, home in 1856-57 to Edward John Cobbett (1815-

1899), a genre and landscape painter who exhibited at the Royal Academy between 1833 and 1880. The four tiny houses of a short-lived Williams Terrace, opposite No.23, also fell victim to the railway. The semi-detached villas across the road (**Nos.52-60**) survive from the mid-1840s, when they were erected by the local builder J Pierce. In 1976 No.50 (alongside the railway viaduct) was opened as an "anti-showhouse" to show the conditions then prevalent in rented property in Camden. It was demolished soon afterwards. The same fate befell the terraced housing on this side (renumbered Nos.37-51), after the Council decided it would be too expensive to rehabilitate, replacing it with the present 2-storey dwellings.

Reach **HARTLAND ROAD**. The Buck family originally came from Hartland in North Devon. On the left-hand corner, behind a tall fence, is a small but well-stocked garden centre, on the site of No.51 Hawley Road, which was a baker's for most of its existence. Look left along the road. The south side is recent except for **No.2**, at the far end, now part of the restaurant on the corner of Chalk Farm Road. Nos.4-24 were demolished at the same time as the houses in Hawley Road. The whole block was laid out as a community garden until the present terrace was built in the late 1980s. It faces an original 1840s terrace, now colourfully painted. Before WWI **No.19** was home to Charles Banting, a

dealer in pigeons, which would have been in great demand in what was then a solidly working-class district. Cross over to that side, by the covered driveway between **No. 35** and **No.37**, which leads to a workshop, contemporary with the houses. It now boasts a prominent leaded light, this being the base of the specialist firm Lead & Light, started in the 1970s on a stall in Camden Lock market. Look back across the road at diminutive **No.28**, with its shutters and greenery.

Continue, under the railway arch and briefly into an area that was covered in *Streets of Kentish Town.* Notice on the right, masked by trees, the church of Holy Trinity in whose parish much of this route lies. Holy Trinity, Haverstock Hill was created as a district in 1847 and raised to parish status in 1868. Its spire, damaged in WWII, was removed and not replaced. Shot here were several scenes in the 1947 film *It Always Rains on Sunday,* directed by Robert Hamer and starring Googie Withers as a married woman who shelters her former lover after he escapes from prison. *Camden Celebrates Cinema 100* (1996) includes a still featuring Hartland Road south of the railway bridge; Holy Trinity is in the background, with a decapitated spire. The Camden Plaza advertised the film with "Come and see the film made in this district", although it was set in the East End.

Pass the former Royal Exchange pub and

turn left into **CLARENCE WAY**. Until the early 19th century the Hampstead arm of the River Fleet flowed across open land here, until it was diverted further north. The part of Clarence Way from the junction to the railway arch was only formed when the church school buildings opposite were erected in 1849-50. It opened up the cul-de-sac that lay beyond the railway arch and which had been developed as a side turning out of Harmood Street ahead, known as George Street. In 1885 it was renumbered as part of Clarence Road, which was given its present name of Clarence Way in 1937.

We have now re-entered the former Harmood estate. Records of the Tottenhall Manor show that Henry (Harry) and Mary Harmood, who then lived in Kentish Town, were admitted tenants of the manor for a field here in the early 1800s. This was the 9-acre Shoulder of Mutton Field. In December 1821 Harry Harmood, of Eastbourne, successfully appealed to the Vestry against its rating at a time when he was starting to develop the estate; he had already sold off 5 acres and laid out the first road. The field was almost completely built over during the next 20 years.

Clarence Way is delightful, its tiny terraced houses opening straight onto the pavement and well maintained. As Pevsner and Cherry say, these have a "curious rhythm of rising parapets". The small street, dating mainly from 1843-44, gives a good idea of how much of this part of

West Kentish Town would have appeared in the 1840s. Just before the end of the street, **HARMOOD GROVE** leads off left. On its western side is an interesting old lamp-post, rather askew. Opposite this, the street was once lined with 5 small, terraced houses, here from the 1850s until WWII. At No.1 Alexander Dodson was living with his family in 1881. He was a coach builder employing 22 men in the works alongside that terminate the street.

Retracing our steps, we turn left and shortly join **HARMOOD STREET**, at **No.34**, an end-of-terrace house with its entrance in Clarence Way. Harmood Street was begun in 1821 as the first side turning (in this area) from the main highway leading to Hampstead. Greenwood's 1827 map of London shows houses along the opposite, west side of the street as far as the site of the block of flats to our right. Only Nos.1-11 remain from this first phase. The street was extended during the 1830s and was fully built up by the mid-1840s, except for the site below No.14.

The houses in Harmood Street were small, and although they were initially occupied by middle-class residents, by the 1860s this was a solidly working class street. The houses are now quite fashionable, after a period in the 1960s when they were threatened with demolition. Local residents won out and the street was restored in 1970s, and in 1981 the scheme won a Civic Trust Award.

In 2005 the Council proposed making this street the hub of a Conservation Area.

Turn left. On this side is a terrace at **Nos.14-34** that was originally built as Oliffe Place, a name retained until 1885 when the whole street was renumbered. Many of the houses are ivy-clad, some have wisteria, all are very charming. Beyond them, the site at Nos.2-12 was developed only in the 1860s, as coach building works that stretched through to Harmood Grove. They were occupied by Alexander Dodson until 1893. His son Christopher (1874-1959) then took over and expanded the business. A highly competitive builder of horse buses and cabs in the years before WWI, in the early 1920s he turned to motor buses. He soon ran a fleet of 2,000 so-called "pirate" buses, including the 'Chocolate Express' along Route 11, which were very popular and more comfortable than those run by the monopolistic London General Omnibus Company. He moved his business to Willesden and retired, immensely rich, to Jersey. In the later 1920s the Mohawk Motor Cab and bus services were operated here by Walter Dangerfield. Bombed in WWII and subsequently redeveloped as commercial premises, now demolished, the site is currently used as a car park, entered through the Chalk Farm Service Station (p 21).

Cross over and turn back northwards along the west side of the road. Here **No.1A** is a 3-storey former piano factory dating from the 1870s, refurbished as offices. Note the fancy, sculpted metal grilles. **Nos.1-11** are attractive houses dating from the 1820s. Particularly appealing are Nos.7-11, the earliest in the street, which have round-headed doors and round-headed recesses framing their upper windows. When Nos.9&11 (then Nos.5&6) were up for sale in 1827, they were said to have uninterrupted views towards Hampstead. Their design is echoed in part in **Nos.13-19**, a modern terrace bearing the prominent date of 1995 that also features in two similar terraces at **Nos.21-31** and **Nos.33-39**. The latter lie beyond the gated entrance to modern **COLLARD PLACE,** whose name recalls the famous Camden Town piano firm of Collard & Collard, although it was in neighbouring Augusta Street that Samuel Collard (d.1849), a wealthy Kentish Town landowner, owned houses in the 1820s. Collard Place was built on the site of a large bus garage **[6]**, opened here during WWI as the Chalk Farm depot of the London General Omnibus Company that was subsequently absorbed into London Transport.

On the site of No.39 (then No.20) Harmood Street was a beerhouse known in the 19th century as the Barley Mow. Beyond is a footpath beside **Harmood House**, one of the 5 blocks that make up the **Ferdinand Estate**. The footpath lies

6 Chalk Farm Bus Garage: interior view, 1936

on the line of former Augusta Street, a cul-de-sac begun in 1824-25 at the same time as the earliest houses in Harmood Street. It was lined with 5-roomed houses plus Augusta Cottage, home in 1881 to the master carver, Richard Wethersett. The street was renamed Harmood Place in 1886. Turn left along the footpath, past a striped SPPM (St Pancras Parish, Middlesex) marker post, to get a feel for the Estate, begun in 1935 in the typical St Pancras neo-Georgian style – walk-up blocks in red and grey brick by A J Thomas, the architect of the Town Hall in Euston Road. To your right, the three arms of Harmood House enclose a courtyard. Farther along is a green space enclosed by Harmood House and two further blocks: **Ferdinand House** to your left and **Powlett House** closing the view. The construction of the Estate was held up for nearly a year by a tenant of Harmood Place, Henry Edward Walton, a father of five who refused to move, until the Council took him to court.

Return to **HARMOOD STREET**. Under the grounds of Harmood House to our left lies the site of No.22 (after 1885 No.43), where the naturalist Henry Walter Bates (1825-1892) was living with his family in 1863. This was four years after his return from Amazonia, where he had spent over a decade collecting 14,700 species of insects, animals and birds mostly new to science. He provided the first comprehensive scientific explanation of the phenomenon subsequently known as Batesian mimicry, whereby non-poisonous animals mimic the bright warning colours of poisonous species. Bates was an important advocate of the ideas of Darwin, with whom he maintained a regular correspondence. As the principal official at the Royal Geographical Society from 1864 until his death, he sustained its exploration activities, supporting both Livingstone and Stanley in Africa.

On the opposite side, in a terrace of four original houses, is **No.38**, a shop called Walden Books. Set up by David Tobin in 1979, it takes its name from a book by the American writer Henry Thoreau about getting back to nature and living simply in a log cabin by a lake called Walden Pond. The book's philosophy appealed to Tobin, who stocks second-hand and antiquarian books. Beyond the terrace lies **Chalcot School**. This was opened around 1900 as Harmood Street School, an LCC special school for "mental defectives", which it remained until 1964 when it became an LCC (later ILEA) day school for maladjusted children. It is now a Community Special School catering for 50 boys aged 11-16 with special educational needs. Note the original Girls entrance, marked by a short framed doorway.

Continue past Harmood House to reach another turning into the Ferdinand Estate. On the far corner is **No.57**, until 2001 the Harmood Arms, and converted into flats in 2003 by the Acton Housing Association. The turning is the rump of an early side road, begun as William Street in the 1820s and subsequently called William Street West. In 1865 it was renamed Powlett Place, according to Bebbington a name selected randomly by St Pancras Vestry. In 1886 it subsumed narrow Sussex Passage so as to lead through to Ferdinand Street. It was faced by 19 houses, demolished in the mid-1930s to form the Ferdinand Estate. Booth, visiting in 1898, noted an improvement in the houses over the previous decade and described the occupants as "respectable working-class, nothing against them".

Present-day **POWLETT PLACE** is the cul-de-sac opposite. Cross over, and walk along it. The houses here were first built as William Street Cottages in the 1840s. In 1865 they were renamed as Rilla Place, becoming part of Powlett Place in 1885. They form a pleasant backwater, with small, boxy 2-storey Victorian cottages and well-tended front gardens. Halfway down on the right is a modern infill building, which was built over the entrance to a former London City Mission Hall. Founded in the 1880s, the Camden Town branch of the London City Mission was listed in 1892 at No.15 Harmood Street, but had moved here by 1900. The mission was led until 1921 by George Green, who lived at No.62 Harmood Street and had his own private entrance into the Hall, which was constructed in his garden over the site of an ornamental fountain. After his retirement, the Mission Hall ceased to function as such, although the Chalk Farm Salvation Army Band (p 19) still practised here. In the 1950s, by which time the Hall was being used as a workshop, the owner of the timber yard behind Nos.62-64 Harmood Street applied unsuccessfully for an access road to run down Powlett Place. In the next decade the playground of Chalcot School was extended over part of the timber yard, which together with the former Mission Hall was left with no access. In 1976 the Council planned to lay out the land as a communal garden reached by a footpath from Powlett Place. Instead, the present house was built with the land used as its garden, in which an old fireplace complete with flue and chimney from the old Hall remains. Powlett Place ends at the railway line and (left) the gates of Castle Road.

Returning to **HARMOOD STREET**, turn right and continue walking northwards. On this east side the houses are 2-storey, with the same round-arched doorways that we saw at the southern end of the street. Opposite, the houses are also 2-storey but some have stucco window surrounds; mainly dating from 1843, on the first floor they contained 3 bedrooms and a servant's room. The three storeys of **No.65** break the skyline of the terrace. An archway once led to a factory built in the early 1890s on

the backland between Harmood Street and Little Charles Place, first used by the piano maker W G Wernam and adjoining Cremmen's coach-building works (p 30). There was a factory here until the 1970s; the path now leads into Mutton Place (p 31).

Also 3-storey are the 4 former shops at **Nos.102-108** that terminate the street on this side. These were built at the end of the 1840s when Harmood Street – until then a cul-de-sac – was pushed through beyond the Harmood estate boundary to meet Prince of Wales Road ahead. In the 1890s at **No. 104** was one of only two common lodging houses in Kentish Town, which Booth in 1898 described as well-conducted, with beds at 4d or 6d a night. At that time, such lodging houses were under direct and continual police supervision, every room being inspected before occupation.

We reach **PRINCE OF WALES ROAD** where we pause. We have now re-joined the former Southampton estate. Over it, Prince of Wales Road was first projected in 1840, but not formally named as such until 1863, when all of its various terraces were renumbered. The road was renumbered again in 1886. By then, it was a busy thoroughfare, lined with shops as well as dwellings.

Unlike its modern neighbours, the **Prince of Wales** pub on the corner dates from the 1840s. The stuccoed 3-storey building retains late-Victorian brown tiling at ground level. In August 2002, at the Old

Bailey, the former pop star Adam Ant (real name Stuart Goddard) was placed under a 12-month community rehabilitation order, following an incident in which he threatened drinkers at the pub with a starting pistol, after they had mocked his "cowboy" clothes. He had smashed the pub's windows and injured a pub musician.

Walk towards the railway bridge, right. Beyond the pub lay the top of one of Messrs Bassett's brickfields, which was not developed until 1860. Today, an early-1980s red-brick block, **Nos.57-61D** and **Nos.63A-63D**, fronts the road. It has an asymmetric design, featuring a prominent staircase. At the end of the block, just before the railway bridge, turn right up steps along a footpath leading to a leafy housing development built at the same time. This is numbered as part of **CASTLE ROAD** and lies over the site of houses dating from the early 1860s that were built on the brickfield. Just past **Nos.139-161** pause under a large plane tree and look left through the railway arch along the road, which began as a turning off Kentish Town Road (visible in the distance) and takes its name from the famous old Castle Tavern, pulled down in 1848, over whose grounds its runs. Until 1864 the street was called New Hampstead Road, and had several individually named terraces along it; here the houses were first called Taunton Terrace, after the builder James Taunton, whose firm was based in the railway arches.

Alongside the railway viaduct is **CASTLE MEWS**. Before WWI this was the base for several forage dealers or manure merchants; and here from 1865 to 1904 was the piano factory of the London Pianoforte Company, who used the name "Dussek and Dussek" referring to famous Czech pianist Jan and his London-born organist daughter Olivia Dussek (1801-1847); its offices were in Lyme Street, Camden Town. This building was later taken over by Buttle's, founded here in 1919 by George Harold Buttle, grandfather of the present managing director. The firm supplies timber, building materials and tools. In May 2003 the local press reported that this family-run business was among ten firms under threat of being pushed out by a tide of "trendy" high-tech offices that Spacia, the commercial property arm of Network Rail, wished to build underneath the railway viaduct between Camden Town and Gospel Oak. To date, this has not materialised.

Retrace your steps to regain **PRINCE OF WALES ROAD**, and cross over by the zebra crossing to its north side by Talacre Gardens (p 53) and turn left. Pause by the corner of Talacre Road to view the buildings on the opposite side. Beyond Harmood Street is another low, continuous 1980s brick block, **Nos.1-12 and Nos.13-24 Mutton Place**. It covers the very broad entrance to former Prince of Wales Crescent which until the late 1970s curved round to this point from the top of Ferdinand Street (see map on p 2). The Crescent was begun in 1843 and was known until 1865 by the name of individual terraces along it – Queen's Crescent on the north side, facing Sussex Terrace and Charles Place (Charles Fitzroy (1804-1872 was the 3rd Lord Southampton who sold the estate in 1840). The houses were compact 3-storey dwellings and almost from the first there were many shops. Booth, in 1898, described the Crescent as "rather rough". In the middle of Charles Place was an entry to the even lowlier Little Charles Place, which was very poor from the start. In the 1880s prostitutes were said to operate from a number of its houses, although the 1881 census unsurprisingly gives no hint of this; most of the woman are described as laundresses. Booth also records that "a sad-looking cretin child here grinned vacantly to himself, but he was not in rags – only rather untidy". Little Charles Place became Charles Close in 1938. Between Little Charles Place and Harmood Street, at No.15 Prince of Wales Crescent, was the coach-building works of Daniel Cremmen. In 1890 he invented a 'safety omnibus' that prevented overturning if a wheel or axle broke.

At No.26 Prince of Wales Crescent, Stephen Samuel Wales ran a fancy goods shop. In May 1867 he was sentenced to 10 years' penal servitude for attempting to defraud the Western Insurance Office: he was adjudged to have started deliberately the fire above his shop. The case was interesting for the various eminent chemistry experts who hypothesised about the substance used to start the blaze.

Camden Council's plans in the 1970s to demolish Prince of Wales Crescent caused an outcry, even being discussed in the national press. The houses could easily have been rehabilitated but were left to decay. From 1971 more and more properties fell empty and a lively community of squatters on short-term licences moved in. Artists and filmmakers among them attempted in 1974 to save the Dairy at No.11 by recreating its old farmyard scene in a theatrical show. But the Dairy was demolished in 1976 and the other houses followed. The street was closed and removed in 1977.

The Mutton Place block also lies over former No.79 Prince of Wales Road, home before WWI to Benjamin Phelps, whose family ran the Kentish Town-based Phelps piano-making company; it had a base here until the 1930s. Beyond at **Nos.83-85** is a rather dilapidated 5-storey block of flats built in 1965 and called Van Bern House. It is the base for the Iroko Foundation, a small UK-based charity established to support initiatives in Africa for the conservation of forests and wildlife by rural people. The building lies over part of former Albert Terrace, 3 of whose semi-detached villas have survived at Nos.87-97. The first surviving pair, **Nos.87-89**, now houses the Prince of Wales Group Practice. This has been a doctor's surgery since 1976, following a move from No.99 on the corner ahead.

Meanwhile, on the north side of Prince of Wales Road, cross Talacre Road and reach a long 3-storey terrace beyond at Nos.92-132 and stretching as far as Malden Road (p 57). **No.92** on the corner has stucco embellishments, but also a rather unattractive modern roof extension. It is now the Skyros Centre, a retreat which organises "alternative" holidays in Greece. According to founder Dina Glouberman, Skyros is a total living experience and Europe's first centre of this kind, offering over 250 courses ranging from abseiling to yoga, massage and spirituality. Nos.92-110 were begun in the mid-1840s as Hollis Place, a name retained until 1863 and which probably derived from Hollis Cottage by the Eschol Nursery (p 55). In the 1850s **No.94** (then No.2 Hollis Place) was a school for six young gentlemen run by Mr Guy, who had been preceptor in the Duke of Wellington's family. **No.96** was home in 1887-89 to the photographer George William Roberts. At **No.108** (then No.9 Hollis Place), Miles Edmund Cotman (1810-1858), watercolour painter and the eldest child of the more famous artist John Sell Cotman, was living from 1851 to 1854, when ill-health led him to move back to his

native Norfolk. His subjects were Norfolk landscapes and river and sea views; there is a major collection of his work in Norwich Castle Museum. At **No.110** (No.10), the naturalist Henry Bates (p 28) was staying in January 1863 at the time of his marriage and before moving to Harmood Street. Also original is the front door at **No.102**. Some of the unusual first-floor balconettes have survived, as have the spear-headed area railings. The latter are continued in front of **Nos.112-132**, which date from the early 1850s and are slightly taller than their neighbours.

Carefully cross over to the south side of the road and return to Harmood Street, then turn right into **MUTTON PLACE**. This was developed over Prince of Wales Crescent in 1980-81. The name comes from the once adjacent Shoulder of Mutton Field. Walk alongside the block at **Nos.36-48** to the end of the service road. Turn left into another part of the Estate, a square formed of more low brick blocks, whose hard edges are softened by the many trees; the landscaping is by Michael Brown Partnership. This is **FORGE PLACE**. Take the exit path that is diagonally opposite and continue walking with the block at Nos.39-49 on your left until you emerge by the side of a large building site. Here, from the early 19th century, stood the eponymous forge, listed as Smith's Cottage on the 1841 census. It was more recently No.1 Forge Place, which housed

the Harmood Community Centre, home among others to Badejo Arts, a dance company founded in 1990 that blends traditional Nigerian dance with British contemporary dance; the company has now moved to the InterChange Studios at the old Hampstead Town Hall on Haverstock Hill. A new building to house a community hall, nursery, day-care and family support facilities, as well as a charity and a Sure Start office is under construction here.

At the end of Forge Place turn left into **FERDINAND STREET**. It was developed on land owned by the Fitzroy family; George Ferdinand Fitzroy (d.1810) was the 2nd Lord Southampton. The street is first shown on Greenwood's map of 1827 as a straight road into fields, with no buildings along it, other than the forge; two entrances led to stables behind Pancras Vale. The first few houses in the street, on the corner of Ferdinand Place ahead, were built in 1831, but the street was mainly developed in the early 1840s after Lord Southampton had sold off his estate. It was renumbered in 1885.

Ferdinand Street quickly became a major thoroughfare, an omnibus route lined with shops. Tram tracks were laid along it by the late 19th century. In the 1930s plans were drawn up to redevelop its housing, which had become very run-down. Apart from Kent House (see below), the blocks along it now are, however, all post-WWII. 8-storey **Beauvale**, on our left, dates from 1950. Its name has an historical connection, in common with other St Pancras Council blocks in the area erected at this time: during the 15th century a rent was paid to the Prior of Beauvale (Notts.) from part of Tottenhall Manor, within whose historical boundaries Ferdinand Street now lies. Beauvale replaced a long row of shops, including No.64 (previously No.27) which was home in 1885 to James Lee, alias Adams, alias Manson, who was convicted of the "Romford Murder" of Inspector Thomas Simmonds of the Essex Constabulary. He had to be restrained in court by half a dozen constables.

Continuing past Beauvale, 6-storey **Broomfield** beyond is later, erected in 1964 and looking extraordinarily old-fashioned for that date. Its bricks appear shoddily laid but are in fact mere facing, on concrete. It covers the site of a Victorian beerhouse at No.44 (originally No.17) called the Engineer's Arms, as well as former Nos.34-42. The London Institution for Lost and Starving Cats, founded in Hampstead in 1890 by Mrs Morgan, moved here in 1900. Mrs Morgan's real name was Zoe Constance Marie de Longueville. She married Captain J K Ruttledge of the 2nd Dragoon Guards and spent thousands of pounds of their money on the institution, which otherwise depended on charity. It used the prefix 'Royal' from 1901 to 1910 when it enjoyed the patronage of Queen Alexandra. The institution collected stray cats (and from 1902 dogs as well) in its horse-drawn van. The huge number of unwanted cats – they arrived at the rate of 60-80 each day – meant that most had to be destroyed within 24 hours. Many were already beyond saving due to starvation, disease or injury and these were destroyed at once, in a lethal box capable of holding twelve animals at a time. In 1901 Mrs Morgan advertised that "we search everywhere for lost and starving cats and in default of a home end their miserable lives by chloroform". The service was free to the poor and, apparently, no gratuities were allowed. Posters depicted its staff in formal nurses' uniforms. The institution also provided free medical care to cats whose owners could not afford the attention of a vet.

Mrs Morgan died in 1929 aged 76 and in her will left the institution to Our Dumb Friends League on the understanding that they would maintain the same regime, with no vivisection or experiments upon living animals allowed. Our Dumb Friends League ran the institution until 1957, when the League was taken over by the Blue Cross, based here for just one more year. Mrs Morgan's fund was however still going strong in 1965 when a charity in her name was registered that applied the income towards the upkeep of the Animals Hospital in Victoria.

Continue to the **Crowndale** at No.10 on the corner. In the 1850s there was a beerhouse here called The Hope. This subsequently became the Prince of Wales, probably in the 1860s; when the premises were relicensed in 1888 it was noted that they had been licensed since some time before 1869. The pub changed its name to the Crowndale after WWII, presumably to avoid confusion with its namesake on nearby Prince of Wales Road. The present rather ugly block, with its traditional-style windows, was built in 1966 over the site of the first three houses in the street. These dated from the early 1830s, when they were numbered 1, 2 and 3. At that time they adjoined White's Cottage, home to the builder James Hunt in 1841. It formed part of **FERDINAND PLACE**, into which we turn left.

This L-shaped cul-de-sac was started in the 1830s; on the 1840 sale plan of the Southampton estate there were already 13 houses on its eastern side. It was extended northwards during the 1840s until it reached William Street (later Powlett Place). Census records show it as home to railway workers and labourers and by 1881 to a manure merchant, Joseph Tofield, who later moved to Castle Mews (p 30). In 1885 it was renumbered when it subsumed Sussex Place north of Powlett Place, a row of 12 tiny houses fronting a footpath behind the gardens of Nos.25-63 Prince of Wales Crescent (former Sussex Terrace). The footpath was aligned with Little Charles Place, and divided from it by a fence across the roadway, as noted by Booth in 1898. He also wrote that in Ferdinand Place's varied but very small 2-storey houses there were "a few loose women and larrikin thieves about". When he returned on a Sunday he found nobody but young boys: "there was nothing ragged about them except their morals", because they were looking for a fight.

On Ferdinand Place's western arm today, the right-hand side is taken up by offices, occupying an old sheet metal works that had another entrance at No.46 Chalk Farm Road. Opposite at No.1 is the post-WWI **Crowndale House** (named after the pub), which we follow round the corner; above its entrance note its name supported by a cat and a dog, and surmounted by another. From Victorian times, veterinary surgeons were based both at No.1 and at former No.4 on the corner diagonally opposite. In 1880 the wife of the vet George Augustus Hall killed herself by drinking prussic acid "whilst suffering from temporary insanity brought on by the unkindness and neglect of her husband". In the 1960s a taxidermists operated side by side with the vets, an interesting combination! Since 1970 these buildings have housed the garages of the funeral directors Leverton & Sons (established in 1789), the firm which organised the funerals of Diana, Princess of Wales (1997) and Elizabeth, The Queen Mother (2002). When Leverton's moved in they demolished some old cottages

opposite and built the present large garage for their hearses. They also found it very difficult to remove the smell of cats' urine at Crowndale House. Ferdinand Place now ends abruptly at the grounds of the Ferdinand Estate, and all of its tiny residential buildings have gone. Most of those on the east side (along with the

7 Ferdinand Place Ragged School and Church

former Squire's piano factory) were pulled down to form the Chalk Farm bus garage (p 27), which could be entered from Ferdinand Place. Part of the bus garage's Listed wall remains but its site is now taken by private Collard Place (p 26). Other houses nearer Powlett Place survived until 1935, when they were pulled down to form the Estate ahead. Amongst them stood the Ragged School [7], next to former No.30 (until 1885, No.14). The school was opened in 1850 by the new Church of Holy Trinity in Hartland Road. The simple Gothic structure in polychromatic brick was designed by Mr Moore of Walbrook and erected by local builders Manley & Rogers of Hartland Road. It had a large 1-room interior which was capable of holding 800 people for morning service on Sunday. There were two schools, one for up to 300 boys and another for up to 300 girls (average attendance in the mid-1860s was 174 per day). A soup kitchen was opened alongside, staffed by ladies from Highgate, who in the harsh winter of 1864-5 doled out over

3,000 gallons of soup. The building was used as the Mission Hall of Holy Trinity Church from the 1890s until it was sold in 1907. After WWI it was occupied by an engineering company before its eventual demolition.

Returning to **FERDINAND STREET**, note to our left the shops at **Nos.2–8**, which date from the 1840s. No.6 has a tiny grille at the front. Cross over to a small row of shops opposite and turn right. Ahead on our left is the once daringly modern **Kent House**, built by the St Pancras House Improvement Society in 1935 to the designs of Colin Lucas, with Amyas Connell and Basil Ward. There are 16 flats in two 5-storey blocks, which have a concrete frame, and which were in the forefront of contemporary, Modernist design when they were built. They were named after the Duke of Kent, who took a keen interest in social housing and who visited the building in December 1935, a few weeks after it had opened. The flats were let at affordable rents yet had a quality of finish normally only seen in private commissions. There was a direct staircase to each pair of flats to avoid the gallery approach, already a source of complaints. New gates and landscaping were undertaken in 1982 by Jeffrey Fairweather and the blocks were repaired in 2005.

Next to Kent House, a side turning that originally led to the grounds of Cumberland Lodge (p 20) now leads to a yard containing commercial properties at **Nos.19&21**. These occupy part of a Victorian piano works that was home to Chappell & Co (p 38), who were listed in directories at No.19.

Beyond the turning, and facing the road, are two blocks of post-war **Ferdinand Street Estate** – **Tottenhall** and **Rugmere** – named after two of the manors that made up medieval St Pancras. The blocks are separated by playgrounds from the third block which lies back; this is **Mead Close**, named after a nearby field. These monumental 8-storey buildings, with neo-Georgian doorcases, date from 1946; Rugmere mirrors its contemporary, Beauvale, across the street. The Estate covers the site of 3 cul-de-sacs developed in the 1840s, which soon deteriorated, but survived until bombed in WWII. From south to north these were Haverstock Place, Haverstock Street and Hethersett Street. Haverstock Place, whose houses were let to weekly tenants, had a public house on its southern corner with Ferdinand Street. Known in the 19th century as the London & North Western, the pub lost its licence in 1903. Five years earlier Booth described the inhabitants of Haverstock Street as "very low class, rowdy at night", but he reserved his opprobrium for Hethersett Street, to the north, which he said had a stricken appearance because of drink. He wrote that there were no convicted criminals, only "youngsters who do a snatch and run". A different picture emerges from the 1886 court case involving the 13-year-old inhabitant Mary Travel, who was arrested for begging; she had been forced to do this because the landlord had seized her father's means of livelihood, his pony and trap from which he sold vegetables, in lieu of a month's rent, amounting to 22s 6d. The court felt the landlord's action unreasonable.

The top of Ferdinand Street merges into **MALDEN CRESCENT**; the Fitzroy family owned land in Malden, Surrey. It has been almost wholly redeveloped, but once formed the western side of a triangular area. Prince of Wales Crescent (p 30) curved round to the east and at the junction of the two roads was a pub, the British Queen, built in 1846 and surviving until the mid-1970s **[8]**. The third side of the triangle was formed by Albert Terrace (p 30) along Prince of Wales Road.

Before 1863, Malden Crescent was known by the names of the houses along it – on the left-hand (west) side were Eastcott Place, Henman Terrace and short Malden Place, while Victoria Crescent stood opposite. Eastcott Place comprised 3 pairs of large, semi-detached villas built in the early 1840s, with very long back gardens. It may have been named after Richard Eastcott, who was the Surgeon Apothecary at St Pancras Workhouse until his resignation in 1843. At No.1 Eastcott Place, Sir George Scharf (1820-1895)

was living in the 1850s. He was the elder son of the artist George Johann Scharf (1788-1860), who taught him to draw. In the 1840s the younger George went on a number of expeditions to Asia Minor, and several books on classical antiquities were later published with his illustrations. In 1857 Scharf was appointed the first Secretary of the newly formed National Portrait Gallery, a post he held until he was made its Director in 1882. In 1860 he moved to live 'over the shop' at the Gallery (then based in Great George Street, Westminster). Next door, at No.2 Eastcott Place, Rev. Thomas King was living with his family and 3 servants in 1851. He was a curate of the new Holy Trinity Church.

Former No.5 (as No.9 Malden Crescent) was home in 1878 to Henry Pope, a singer with the Carl Rosa Opera Company. He appeared in bass roles in the first English performances of several of Wagner's operas during the 1880s.

Immediately north of Eastcott Place lay Henman Terrace, named after Charles Henman who bought the 1½ acre site in 1841 and was living at No.4 from 1844 for at least a decade. Henman was an architect who designed Kingston-upon-Thames Town Hall (now Market House); his son Charles, the architect of Croydon Town Hall, was born here on 30 December 1844. Henman Terrace was bisected by a roadway leading to an undeveloped plot of

land behind. This was not built upon until 1880 when an imposing 5-storey structure with 40,000 sq ft of floor space, designed by Ebbetts and Cobb at a cost of nearly £20,000, was opened there. It had been commissioned by George Rowney & Co to house its factory [9].

The company, established in 1783, and famous for artists' colours, brought about many improvements in the manufacture and production of oil and watercolour throughout its time here, which lasted until 1967, when it moved to Bracknell.

The factory, known as the Malden Works, was ranged in distinct blocks around three sides of a yard. This housed a number of other industrial concerns: in the late 1880s the Electric Traction Company, which failed in its attempt to persuade the Metropolitan Railway to use its Battery Locomotives; and in the 1890s both Blondeau et Cie, perfumiers and makers of Vinolia soap, and Immisch & Co, makers of electric canoes and launches. Moritz Immisch, a German-born clockmaker turned electrical engineer, pioneered the production of battery-powered riverboats. In 1887, with William Coutts Keppel (Viscount Bury), he had set up the world's first electric hire-boat fleet on the Thames.

When the Immisch works here closed down in June 1896, Richard Jordan bought

up much of the machinery and rented the block. The Works became the focus of a scam whereby he and others attempted to raise capital on a new company, Thomas Edward Brinsmead & Sons (Limited), set up to purchase a business of similar name, which had gone into liquidation. Brinsmead had been employed by John Brinsmead and Sons as a mechanic on weekly wages but left in 1894 and started piano making with his two sons in Bartholomew Road, Kentish Town, in very small premises and at no profit. The prospectus for his new company claimed that he was expanding into the Malden Works because he could not cope with demand since he had orders for 800 pianos. In fact, the new company only made 83 pianos in the few months that it operated. T E Brinsmead was clearly trading on the name of the more famous piano company, which obtained an injunction restraining him from continuing to deceive the public. In December 1896 an order was made to wind up the new company, and everyone who had invested in it lost money. The Official Receiver was unable to find the books and accounts of Brinsmead and his two sons who, with Jordan and others, were imprisoned for fraud.

Abutting the entrance to Malden Works was No.21 (previously No.5 Henman Terrace), where Stella Gibbons (1902-89) **[10]** was born and where her father had a medical practice and a dispensary. He was a difficult man, unfaithful to his wife with a succession of governesses. To avoid the constant family rows, Stella spent much of her childhood playing solitary games in her attic room. She was educated at home and then sent to the North London Collegiate School for Girls. Her comic classic, *Cold Comfort Farm* (1932), was written as a parody of the novels of D H Lawrence and Mary Webb, with asterisks marking all the purple passages for the reader's delectation and mirth. Her characters soon became household names and her heroine, Flora Poste, a synonym for common sense.

Beyond Henman Terrace were the four houses of Malden Place, from 1863 Nos.29-35 Malden Crescent. During the 1860s No.1 Malden Place was home to Dr Henry Guard Knaggs, who spent 40 years in practice in Camden Town and was also a noted entomologist and lepidopterist.

All the foregoing villas and terraces in Malden Crescent are now covered by the large Estate called **Denton**, laid out at the end of the 1960s and a good example of the comprehensive redevelopment then much in vogue, which obliterated old street layouts in favour of a series of blocks. Denton's are polygonal, while a tall tower marks the corner with Prince of Wales Road. The Estate is inward-looking, discouraging intrusion by outsiders. Its tenants took Camden Council to court in 1987 and won compensation for perennial winter heating problems.

By the time Denton was completed in 1972 the pendulum had swung in favour of rehabilitating older buildings and the two villas opposite, just before the traffic lights, were saved from demolition. These semi-detached villas, at **No.20** and **No.99 Prince of Wales Road**, were part of a row of similar houses that made up Victoria Crescent (from 1863 part of Malden Crescent) which were otherwise replaced by a red-brick block (**Nos. 22-44**) and others numbered as part of Forge Place. The villas were built a few years after the sale of the Southampton estate in 1840, the original plan of which shows a projected, much grander villa in spacious grounds at this point. Attached to No.99 is a delightful little stucco building with fancy window surrounds. Built in the 1840s, a succession of physicians and surgeons have since lived here, including Benjamin Baillie (1813-1889), who was professionally involved in numerous local inquests, including that of Septimus Hopkins (p 21).

Rejoin Prince of Wales Road, following the edge of Denton. The footpath running left into the Estate is roughly on the line of Roxburgh Grove built in 1852 as a cul-de-sac lined on each side by three detached, 7-roomed villas, with gardens front and back. By the mid-1860s, Roxburgh Grove was connected at its southern end to Belmont Street, which we will shortly visit and as part of which it was renumbered in 1885. Lining the main road either side of Roxburgh Grove was a portion of Roxburgh Terrace, begun in 1850 and renumbered in 1863 as Nos.89-117 Prince of Wales Road. At that time, the piano manufacturer George Youatt was living at No.105; he had a business at 128 Regent's Park Road until 1892.

Continue to skirt the boundary of Denton, turning left into Crogsland Road (p 55). On the far side of the block prominently marked Denton, take the first footpath left and shortly turn right into the western arm of **BELMONT STREET**. This took its name from Belmont House (p 20) over whose grounds it was laid out from 1861. It used to continue left over the site of Denton to join up with former Roxburgh Grove, part of which was pulled down to form No.67, a large (25,000 sq ft) piano factory and showrooms of E Bishop & Sons, established in 1862 and in business here until 1900. The firm's founder and managing director, Edgar Wallace Bishop, had previously worked for Collard & Collard and was imprisoned for 12 months in 1870 for forging the more famous company's mark on his pianos. The business did not survive his death. The factory was taken over by the British Braziery Company. There was a spectacular fire at its premises in June 1916; 18 fire engines and 120 men were needed to quell the flames. In the 1930s A C Shoppee Ltd was manufacturing the Belmont Personal Weighing Machine here.

Farther along on our right is the **Charlie Ratchford Community Centre**, named after the late Councillor, twice mayor of St Pancras and Leader of the Council in the 1960s. The Camden Choir, founded 1971, rehearse here every week and Westminster Kingsway College run classes. Opposite

is an 11-storey block of flats called **Hardington**, built in the early 1960s. These buildings supplanted residential 3-storey houses that Booth in 1898 said were in good repair and generally let in floors to the respectable working-class. Past the late-1970s Camden Council terraced housing at **Nos.13-29**, two of the original houses flank the street, where its two arms meet. Both are stuccoed, although **No.11** appears somewhat drab compared to **No.8** (opposite).

Cross over to the latter and follow the street's eastern arm round the corner. Here at **No.10A** is a very large 3-storey block resembling a Northern textile mill. It was built as Chappell's piano factory. Founded in 1811, and originally music publishers, Chappell's began in 1840 to produce their own pianos. They opened a works in Soho, but as the popularity of Chappell pianos grew, they moved in 1860 to a new factory here, subsequently enlarging it many times. The composer Richard Strauss wrote to the company that its piano had a "remarkable sweet and sympathetic" tone. In 1901 Chappell Piano Co. Ltd was incorporated as a company separate from the music publishing business, and in 1922 production of grands and uprights reached one hundred a week. In 1929 Chappell expanded and acquired Collard & Collard. Until WWII it maintained a showroom, using the Collard name, at adjoining No. 66 Chalk Farm Road. The Belmont Street factory closed down in 1972, and Chappell pianos were last made, by Kemble, in April 2000. Much of the block is at present empty, awaiting new tenants; its present occupants are the SBZ food company and the Austrian Sausage Centre.

Beyond, on the door of the ordinary-looking house at **No.10**, a discreet bronze plaque announces it as the London Zendo Centre. Besides a temple, with worship in the Rinzai Zen tradition, it houses a resident monk. At the end of the short row of houses is a gated entrance to Mead Close on the Ferdinand Street Estate, which was built over Nos.16-34 Belmont Street after war-time bombing.

Retrace your steps to No.8 and turn left along the last part of Belmont Street. This short stretch was the first to be built in early 1861, after the demolition of No.15 Caroline Place. It was at first called Caroline Road, but the Belmont name was adopted in 1864 when the two arms we have traversed were begun over the grounds of Belmont House (p 20). The entrance to the Bavarian Brewery (p 19) was on the right-hand side of the street before Bartok, the former Belmont Tavern; note its ivy-shaped first-floor balconettes. Here we rejoin Chalk Farm Road. Turn right and cross the main road by the traffic lights, to reach Chalk Farm Underground station and the end of this walk.

Route 2
Talacre Gardens to Queen's Crescent Market
Sinuous circular walk from Kentish Town West station

For modern map see back cover

We begin this walk at Kentish Town West station on Silverlink Metro's North London Line. Known until 1923 simply as 'Kentish Town', it was opened on the Hampstead Junction Railway (HJR) on 1 April 1867, some seven years after the line itself. The station, with its wooden platforms, was twice destroyed by fire, first in August 1872 and again, almost a century later, in April 1971. Closed for a decade, it was rebuilt with Greater London Council funding and re-opened by Ken Livingstone, then GLC leader and currently Mayor of London.

Outside the station, glance to the east, beneath the arched railway bridge along **PRINCE OF WALES ROAD** (see also pp 29 & 57). On the left, just outside our area, are the six still-occupied houses of former Claremont Terrace, which was built in the later 1840s and whose name was abolished in 1863. It was soon to be bisected by the viaduct of the HJR. Turn west, past the remains of an earlier station building and bricked-up No.52,

another Claremont Terrace survival on the corner beyond. Cross Dalby Street (p 54) and continue along the southern edge of Talacre Gardens (p 53). Here the western part of Claremont Terrace lined the main road until c.1979, when it was demolished to make way for the new open space.

Born here at No.21 in 1859 was Rev. John Wakeford, a police sergeant's son who, after pastoral work among the poor of Liverpool, rose to become a canon of Lincoln Cathedral. His fervent Anglo-Catholicism made him enemies in the Church. In 1921 he was found guilty by a consistory court on charges of adultery, trumped up (he claimed) by a fellow clergyman with a grudge. Wakeford's unsuccessful appeal to the Privy Council aroused great public excitement, but the legal costs bankrupted him and he died nine years later in an asylum in Kent.

Turn right up **TALACRE ROAD**. The 3-storey terrace at **Nos.3-9** on the left is the oldest on this walk, erected by 1849, while **Nos.11-23** are somewhat later. This was originally Weedington Street. Thomas Weeding, who purchased land here from the Southampton estate, was a wealthy City merchant, of Malden (Surrey), who invested heavily in local property before his death in 1856. He was a churchwarden in 1819-20. The '-ton' suffix appended to his surname suggests that he may have envisaged the area becoming known as 'Weeding Town'. Although this was not to be, his family is recalled in the name of present-day Weedington Road (p 44) and indirectly in that of Newbury Mews (p 58).

On the east side of Talacre Road, now empty of buildings and lining the open space, Victorian housing later gave way to industry. Before and after WWII erstwhile No.20 was shared by the Snooker Ball Company and John Nidd, a maker of billiard cues. Post-war occupants at Nos.14-18 included the organotherapy chemists Richter Gedeon and the Pharmaceutical Trust Ltd; while Selsdon Plastics manufactured "ball-pointed pens", Freedex Ltd made handbags and Fermark created brassières.

Scarcely an asset to the present streetscape is the single-storey glorified shed on the west side at Nos.25-27. Named the **Pat Newman Centre** (after a boxer), this was erected in 1984 as a new gym for the St Pancras Amateur Boxing Club, also known as the St Pancras Boys' Club, and previously housed in the Lyndhurst Hall (p 45). Founded in 1900 by Harry Webster, the club led a peripatetic existence, migrating north from King's Cross via Camden Town before settling here. It has been a training ground for numerous ABA champions. George Francis, born in Camden Town and a 28-times champion, become personal trainer to Frank Bruno. When Camden Council funding for the new Talacre Road premises ran out, local businesses stepped into the breach. Today,

the recently renamed Kronk St Pancras Amateur Boxing Club is under the auspices of the international Kronk boxing empire based in Detroit.

Cross Marsden Street (p 60). Routine modern social housing on the corner at **No.35** occupies the site of the Prince Albert public house, which had a theatre licence in 1856-63. It was briefly renamed the Rose of England in the 1990s before its eventual closure. Continue to the next corner and to the more imaginative post-modern **No.47** there, designed (c.1989) by David Baker in red and yellow brick for a housing association. Cherry & Pevsner note its "pedimented gable ending, echoing the Italianate sources of the C19 housing". Examples of the latter remain, sandwiched between the two more recent buildings at **Nos.41-45**. As early as 1865, No.45 had become home to a working men's club, while neighbouring No.37 was listed as a 'Public Soup Kitchen'.

Look across to the right, and to white, creeper-clad 'Solar House' at **Nos.50-56** Talacre Road, actually on the north side of the ingress to Wilkin Street (p 51). Dating from 1996, the irregularly shaped house has a touch of the medieval about it, but was designed to be eco-friendly, solar-powered and with an insulating turf roof. The latter caused problems at the planning-application stage: neighbours were concerned that when the owner mowed his lawn, he would be looking

directly into their upstairs windows. To allay their fears, rabbits were installed on the roof to keep the grass down. The story attracted international press coverage, which led to the owner receiving a letter from Chile warning that the rabbits risked being plucked from the roof by eagles!

In 1863 Thomas Weeding's Weedington Street had become the southern end of a once longer Weedington Road, which extended northwards as far as former Hanover Street (p 92). The 1960s West Kentish Town housing estate (up ahead) severed the road's later northern stretches from its original south end, which Camden Council renamed Talacre Road, after a North Wales village on the Flintshire coast seven miles east of Rhyl.

Turn left along **RHYL STREET**, which gained its own Welsh name a century earlier in 1865, when renamed by St Pancras Vestry. Seaside resorts were then a popular source of street names for the Vestrymen, who may have been further influenced by the proximity of Prince of *Wales* Road. Early houses in Rhyl Street were known as Murray Terrace, while the road itself was at first called Murray Street. Development had begun soon after 1860 at this eastern end of the street, where **Nos.1-5** survive. No.1 was host in 1873 to meetings of the Wesleyan Reform Union. From the 1880s until after WWII, demolished Nos.4-8 opposite housed the London Domestic Mission of the

Unitarians. Most early Rhyl Street residents were in trade; two laundresses were among them; the ratepayer of a house and workshops at No.16 on the north side was in 1870 the builder and Vestryman Samuel Lamble (see p 87). **Cannington**, on the site today and dating from 1965, is the most south-westerly building of Camden Council's West Kentish Town Estate and the first of many similar blocks that we shall encounter, all named after villages in Somerset.

A further row of original houses remains further west at **Nos.33-39**, identical in style to Nos.42-58 in Malden Road, beyond which thoroughfare the Rhyl Street name was extended in 1886, absorbing former Duke's Terrace (p 61). Intervening south-side houses were pulled down to make way for Rhyl Street Board School, opened by the London School Board in 1898. Still in use, as **Rhyl Primary School**, the classically symmetrical, rather intimidating building has a pitched slate roof with twin spires, invisible from this side. The sash windows are said to be (unusually) original. Infants were at first educated on the ground floor, with junior girls on the first floor and boys on the second. Charles Booth, in 1898, watched pupils leaving the newly completed school. He "saw none unshod; very few ragged; none ophthalmic, and did not detect signs of pinched and hungry faces"; the "level here", he wrote, was "surprisingly high."

On the now grassy corner opposite the school stood the Murray Arms, a beershop turned pub that traded until after WWII. Here turn north up **BASSETT STREET**. A further product of the 1860s, this was known as Winchester Street until 1867, when it assumed the name of George Bassett, surveyor and land agent to Lord Southampton. Land here had been leased to him ten years earlier by Thomas Weeding's widow, Mary. Behind demolished No.2, on the site to your right, were industrial buildings that in the 1870s housed the Economic Gas Range & Roaster Co., oven manufacturers.

A continuous terrace of 3-storey, part-stuccoed houses with small front gardens lines the west side of the street at **Nos.1-59**, interrupted only by a boldly and unusually porticoed No.21. Pause here to consider its complicated past. Erected c.1863, it was first used for worship by the Wesleyans, displaced from their chapel in Highgate Road (Wesleyan Place) by the advent of the Midland Railway. The congregation grew, and after only 4 years, moved on again to the much larger church they built in Prince of Wales Road (p 67). No.11 Winchester Street, as it then still was, doubled from the start as a temperance hall, and was listed as such in ratebooks of 1865. Grandly named the Albert Hall – several years before the opening of a namesake in Kensington Gore! – the building housed the local lodge of the International Order of Good

Templars (IOGT), a temperance body, favouring prohibition, that was founded c.1852 in the USA and spread to England in the following decade. The teetotallers subsequently moved to Wilkin Street (p 53), where they established an Albert Lodge. In 1867 the Bassett Street hall-cum-church was leased to a Strict Baptist congregation, the 'Gospel Oak' Baptist Church, which had previously worshipped in Grange Road (p 23). The minister in 1872 was Rev. Martin H Wilkin, probably related to Miss Wilkin, the local school proprietrix (see p 53). In 1878 they were joined by a second Baptist congregation, from Bloomsbury, and the Albert Hall became known as the Keppel Street Memorial Church. A further merger took place in 1903, with the Peniel congregation from Chalk Farm. In the 1930s the church closed, some of its members transferring to the Highgate Road Chapel. A Mr J B Collin bought the premises for a group of Highgate Road young men involved with the local Ragged School mission, which then moved here from its railway arch in Wilkin Mews (p 51). No.21 has served since the 1970s as **Kentish Town Evangelical Church**.

COITY ROAD, opposite, was the west end of Warden Road until 1965, and the nine surviving houses on the north side at Nos.40-56, some with round-arched porches, retain their old Warden Road numbers. Although the South Wales place-name evidently echoes the North Wales name of nearby Rhyl Street, it has not hitherto been adequately explained. We propose a coal-mining connection, with Coity Pit at Blaenavon, part of the Big Pit complex that is now a museum. The village after which neighbouring Talacre Road was named is not only near Rhyl, but was also a coal-mining community; while the blocks on Camden Council's 1960s Curnock Estate in Camden Town were named after mining villages in Yorkshire, inspired perhaps by the local presence, on Euston Road, of the National Union of Mineworkers' HQ.

Walk on up **BASSETT STREET**, past a patch of garden on the right, once a stable yard used by a succession of cowkeepers, the last of whom, a Mrs Watkin, was still listed here as such in 1914. Fronting the yard was former No.8, home in the 1870s to the ladies' school of Mrs Elizabeth Haddock. Beyond here today, at **Nos.6-32**, is a modern brick 'terrace', with a long projecting glazed balcony, designed in 1977 by Castle, Park, Hook and Partners.

On reaching **QUEEN'S CRESCENT,** pause again. This straight part of the street was the last part to be built, shown on an 1862 map as laid out but not yet developed. It borrowed its name from the road's curved earlier-built western end, beyond the green metal 'arch' (to your left) that proclaims the entrance from Malden Road into Queen's Crescent Market. Once a local

shopping street par excellence, the Crescent is still the neighbourhood's commercial heart, although but a shadow of its former self. If you are here on a Saturday, the longstanding street market, with its 77 pitches, will be in full swing. It is not known exactly when the market first started, but it was certainly active by the 1870s. Shop owners once took stalls to increase their selling space, and tradesmen would scramble to bag a pitch when the blowing of a whistle signalled the opening of the market. Before WWII, it was still packed at 8pm on Friday evenings, and after midnight on Saturdays, when, in the days before universal refrigeration, unsold meat was sold off noisily at knock-down prices from stalls lit by oil (and later hurricane) lamps. Locals recall the elderly woman who once sold live eels here, decapitating them on the spot in front of customers.

Though many old shop premises survive, gone are the specialist food outlets of yesteryear, now replaced by businesses reflecting 21st-century lifestyles. Look to the left, where the Costcutters store on the north side occupies premises that before WWII were part of a Woolworths "bazaar" at Nos.122-139; Woolworths, one of several chains with household names that colonised the Crescent, traded here until the 1970s. At **No.58** opposite, the North Western Meat Company sold chilled and frozen meat until 1940. **No.66**, now part of Frank's 'Superstore', was shared

in 1912 by the International Meat Co. and the World Tea Co. No.62, on the same site, was where 40 years earlier the bibliophile Bertram Dobell took over Mrs Toovey's haberdashery and established his first bookshop (see p 66). The modern public toilets on the pavement beyond are successors to underground conveniences beneath the roadway that were deemed an obstruction to market traffic and closed several decades ago.

Turn east along the south side of the street, past the corner shop at **No.74**. Now selling bric-a-brac, this was latterly the butcher's shop of Mr D Cole, whose fascia, red-and-white striped blinds and hanging bull sign still survived in 2005. In the earlier 20th century, the shop belonged to the well-known pork butchers Rayner & King (later, Rayner Ltd **[11]**), who also ran two other shops in the Crescent. Kentish Town was once noted as a great centre of the butchery trade. In 1914, eight butcher's shops were listed in Queen's Crescent, all but one on this south side. Changes of ownership were bewilderingly frequent, and 33 butchery businesses have been identified in the street over time. Three still traded a decade ago, but all are now gone. Before WWII, **No.76** was the shop of tripe dresser Thomas Hale (later Hale & Piper), who also sold pigs' trotters, brains and animal heads; it is now a doctor's surgery. The DIY store at **No.78** was once a Maypole Dairy. **No.86**, another Rayner's branch, which later housed Boots the Chemists, is now an independent pharmacy.

Intersecting from the right is **ALLCROFT ROAD**, which we shall not explore. It began as part of Langford Road, which then ran further north, on the line of Ashdown Crescent, towards Gospel Oak. There it was continued by the original Allcroft Road, named after J D Allcroft, the glove-making financier of St Martin's Church. In 1879 the whole length of Langford Road assumed the name of its northward continuation. Though north of Queen's Crescent it no longer exists, its southern rump preserves the later Allcroft name, now divorced from its historical context. Single-storey **No.47**, on the left, with red-painted brickwork and a pitched roof, houses four commercial units, now boarded up. The architects Burrell Foley Fisher working with the developers Pocket, who help people on low income own their own home, plan to redevelop this site, through to the adjoining street, with 22 prefabricated flats while retaining its existing commercial use. The west side of the road is still lined by a complete 1860s terrace at **Nos.2-44**, stepped down from 3 storeys high at the top end to 2 storeys lower down, many of the houses sporting Corinthian ornament and all with stuccoed window surrounds. Living at No.14 c.1973 was the TV and film actor Terry Scully.

Proceed along the south side of **QUEEN'S CRESCENT**, where No.88A, now part of the Crescent Supermarket, housed the Metropolitan Meat Company in 1912. **No.90**, now selling sportswear and selling Asian garments, was the butcher's shop of Noah Brazil. The William Hill betting-shop opposite, on one corner of Ashdown Crescent (p 97), was until c.2000 the Dreghorn Castle pub. It took its name from a now-demolished 17th-century castle on the outskirts of Edinburgh, built by Sir William Murray, Master of Works to Charles II, who was, perhaps coincidentally, an ancestor of Lord Mansfield, the local (Kenwood) grandee. For a few years after WWI, **No.155** beyond was the 'Meat

11 Rayner Ltd, pork butchers, at No.74 Queen's Crescent: window display c.1926

43

Palace' of butcher R R Warren.

Studio Prints at **No.159** was founded in 1969 to reproduce artists' prints and was initially staffed by three art students. This shop was the nursery, if not the cradle, of one of today's largest supermarket chains. John James Sainsbury and his wife Mary Ann, the daughter of a Somers Town dairyman, opened their first shop in 1869 in Drury Lane. In 1873 the family moved to Queen's Crescent, to live above the branch they opened at No.159. The next census records John and Mary there, with 2 daughters and 4 young sons, who with brothers then as yet unborn each later played a role in managing the embryonic Sainsbury's empire. John Benjamin Sainsbury, a partner in the firm from 1915, later recalled how shoppers once travelled to the Queen's Crescent branch from as far away as Hendon. At No.159 the Sainsburys sold dairy produce and eggs. An 'egg lad' was employed to 'bark' his wares, which were sold from a stall on the pavement outside. At Easter time eggs would be coloured and surrounded by artificial fluffy yellow ducks. A wall-mounted slot machine called a 'mechanical (or iron) cow' dispensed milk to customers when the shop was shut. Noted for its quality of service and attention to hygiene, the early business thrived, and diversified into the sale of bacon and ham. By 1885 the Sainsburys had opened two further shops in the Crescent, one a few doors away at

No.151 (today a convenience store), and the other not quite opposite at **No.98** (now a fish bar also selling kebabs and burgers). A base for the firm's wholesale business was established in nearby, now long-vanished Langford Mews (p 92). The two north-side Sainsbury's shops were both still trading after WWII, the one at No.151 **[12]** surviving until 1968.

Surmounted by four storeys of balconied, pale-brick sheltered housing is **Queen's Crescent Library** at No.165, now with a thriving IT-based Learning Centre. Replacing temporary premises in Athlone Street (p 47), it was opened in May 1978 by Camden Mayor Bob Humphries and Kentish Town author Gillian Tindall. Launched here the next year was *Between the Stacks*, a raunchy novel by library

12 Shop doorway at No.151 Queen's Crescent: inscription lost in refurbishment, 2005

assistant Barry Bowes, set in a north London library.

Shops opposite the library include **No.96**, now an optician's, but once a Home & Colonial store; and on the corner at **No.100**, a branch of the Walton, Hassell & Port grocery chain, now another betting-shop of William Hill. Long-lost shops on the library site were Lipton's grocery at No.161, later Cowan's, a ladies' outfitter; and at No.163 a baker's shop of A B Hemmings, who also had a second shop at No.167 and two more in Malden Road. Today the local bakery is the Regina, some doors ahead on the left, part of a modern shopping parade built in a part of the Crescent that began life as Cavendish Street (p 50).

The brick-built block also houses a **Playcentre**, round the corner to your left, in **WEEDINGTON ROAD**, whose northernmost end will be mentioned in Route 5, and whose historic southern end, now Talacre Road, we described earlier (p 39) with an explanation of its name. Turn south down its onetime middle section, past **No.164**, now being redeveloped, which for decades sold fish, sometimes fresh and at other times fried. Exposed in 2005 was the old fascia of its post-WWII owner, "wet & dry fishmonger" Charles Corby. Suffering "total destruction" during the war were the substantial premises, lower down at Nos.146-158, of lime merchant Gus Davies; he was nonetheless still here three decades later, as a builder's merchant at

Nos.154-158. **No.158** today is the unlikely headquarters of the thriving Kentish Town **Baitul Aman Mosque**, opened in 1999. Though often closed and shuttered, it is a hive of activity on Fridays, when it provides washing facilities for worshippers. So numerous have these become that Friday prayers have been relocated to the Queen's Crescent Community Centre (p 97). The mosque also has an extensive youth programme.

The original houses on the east (left-hand) side, were known as Carlton Terrace until 1863. Later (in 1898) Charles Booth described Weedington Road as "a street with a 'rough' reputation but improved". The houses here, he wrote, were "uniform, stucco, with porticoed entrances – seen by a half light and it might be a street in Bayswater". Some dwellings, however, remained "shabby with the stucco peeling off in a bankrupt sort of way". Past the taxi repair yard at **No.129** (part of the planned redevelopment site mentioned at Allcroft Road), is a very functional 3-storey block housing Nos.121-127.

The road now leads into the centre of the **West Kentish Town Estate**, a comprehensive redevelopment that radically altered the street pattern. In 1958 Sir Leslie Martin (the former LCC architect) had proposed for this area a revolutionary high-density development with internal corridors. His plans were rejected in favour of the rather conventional

estate we see today, mostly comprising 3- or 4-storey flats. They were built by St Pancras Council in 1961-64, using the Reema system, based on storey-high prefabricated panels, the work being supervised by architect William Crabtree. Note, throughout the estate, the drum-like red-brick spiral staircases at the end of each block, intended to soften the impact of the original stark concrete cladding, although this is now hidden behind hanging red tiles. Pass low-rise **Durston** (left) and **Edington** (right), both named after villages in Somerset, the county chosen by the Council as the source for block names in this part of the borough. Ahead and to the left looms 15-storey **Hawkridge**, the Estate's only tower block, named after a place on Exmoor. Hawkridge was evacuated in 1986 when it was belatedly discovered that it had been system-built (and not made of concrete cast on site as was believed). A Ronan Point-style disaster was predicted and repairs were estimated to cost about £4m. In 1988 the Council sold it to a private company; it was purchased in 1991 by University College, London and became student accommodation.

Leaving its original route (straight ahead), present-day Weedington Road does a dog-leg eastward to end prematurely at Warden Road. Follow it round past **Chelwood**. It ends on the line of Carltoun Street, a road of terraced houses now expunged from the map. This began in

the 1850s as Carlton Street, running both north and south of Queen's Crescent, parallel to Carlton (now Grafton) Road (p 50). Early Carlton Street was respectable enough. Two private academies flourished there in 1862: Joseph Whiddon's York House School at No.8 and, nearer Queen's Crescent at No.53, the Tryon House School of Alfred Surrey. No.71 was home to the painter Thomas Earl (fl.1836-1885), whose portrait of the boxer William Thompson is in the National Portrait Gallery. There too is a marble bust of Queen Victoria, created in 1851 by the sculptor Robert Physick (b.1815), who lived for many years at No.20. By the time of Charles Booth's walkabout in 1898, Carlton Street [13] rated only a 'mixed' purple. In 1937 the LCC renamed it Carltoun Street, pronounced 'Cartoon Street' by locals, which name it retained until swept away in the building of the West Kentish Town Estate.

Reach **WARDEN ROAD.** At first called Wellington Street, this was soon renamed, in 1864, supposedly after an unidentified landowner or builder. Opposite stands the **Lyndhurst Hall,** built as a mission hall of the Lyndhurst Road Congregational Church in Hampstead. Started in 1881, in a house in Litcham (now Athlone) Street, the ever expanding mission moved repeatedly, first to larger premises in Preston Street (p 60), then in 1888 to a new 100-seater hall on the corner of

13   Carlton Street c.1904, looking south towards the Lyndhurst Hall, with the corner shop of Thos Hornsby, furniture dealer and 'miscellaneous sales'

Malden Road and Marsden Street. It came to rest in Warden Road, where the 5-storey Lyndhurst Hall was built in 1892 at a cost of £6,000. It was extended through to Litcham Street in 1911, witness a stone laid by Rev. Robert F Horton, the Lyndhurst Road minister for almost 50 years from 1884. A fellow clergyman, Rev. E Shillitoe, served as 'hall warden'. The hall continued to thrive, with a Men's Institute & Club, and other clubs for both sexes and all ages; playing host to the 66th London Boy's Brigade and to the Girl's Life Brigade; and offering the services of a 'Poor Man's

Lawyer'. During WWII it housed a nursery for mothers engaged in war work. Bought in 1962 by St Pancras Council, the building later passed to Camden Council. When, in the 1960s, the peripatetic St Pancras Amateur Boxing Club (see p 40) found a home in the Hall, it was opened by the comedian Norman Wisdom. The Hall served as rehearsal rooms for celebrities of the day, including Gerry & the Pacemakers and the model Twiggy. When the Walker Brothers came to rehearse, Warden Road echoed to the screams of schoolgirl fans assembled outside. The Men's Institute, a

nursery and a pensioners' club continued to flourish into the 1990s until the Hall was closed, deemed underused by Camden Council, which hoped to sell it to a housing association for refurbishment. Once a major focus of local community life, the Lyndhurst Hall stands forlorn and semi-derelict, and in early 2006 awaits demolition by the new owner, the Notting Hill Housing Trust.

Turn right and walk west, with the Hawkridge block on your right. The next turning was once a crossroads where Warden Road, continuing west (see p 41), was intersected by pre-diversion Weedington Road. We now turn down the pedestrianised top end of **TALACRE ROAD**. Until subsumed into Weedington Road in 1863, this section of street was known as Aland Road, a name inspired by the Crimean War and borrowed from the Åland archipelago, in the Baltic, where in 1855 the British fleet destroyed the strategically important Russian fortress of Bomarsund. The Scottish naval commander in charge of the Baltic fleet was Sir Charles Napier. **No.84** on the near corner, and now flats, was for well over a century the Admiral Napier pub. **Langridge** opposite is a further block of the West Kentish Town Estate, with another Somerset name. On the next left-hand corner stood the Star & Garter pub that traded here till after WWII.

Recent pale-brick housing rounds the corner, as do we, into **ATHLONE STREET**. There **Nos.29&30** (left) cover the site of Athlone Street Library, prefabricated by Terrapin Ltd, "built in a day" and opened by Camden Council on 18 November 1967, replacing the earlier West Kentish Town Library in Malden Road (p 61). The temporary structure was in turn replaced in 1978 by the new library in Queen's Crescent.

Initially known as Grafton Street, Athlone Street was built in the 1850s as a tributary of Grafton Road (at its far end). The builder Samuel Lamble, who lived there in 1860 at No.1, also paid rates at many other addresses in the street. Ten years later it was renamed Litcham Street, seemingly after a Norfolk village. Under that name it became a notorious pocket of real poverty in an otherwise 'mixed' area. Coding it dark blue (for 'very poor'), Charles Booth wrote in 1898 of "… houses with broken windows, most doors open, untidy and dirty rather than ragged children, women often slatternly, but not many about". The street, he said, had "a rough drinking and fighting reputation rather than a criminal one".

Three decades later, conditions were no better. There was gross overcrowding:

one ill-lit ground floor housed a family of 13, and one 12-roomed house sheltered 8 families; while many residents spent only 3 shillings a week on food. So reported members of the St Pancras House Improvement Society (SPHIS), later the St Pancras Housing Association (SPHA), which had been formed in Somers Town in 1924 and was then turning its attention to Kentish Town. A St Pancras North Group was established, functioning as a subcommittee of the main organisation. Unlike the Somers Town parent body, over which Father Basil Jellicoe exerted a strong Anglo-Catholic influence, the North Group was run by activists drawn from various denominations. Leading members included Stanley Shaw, a Methodist, and Leonard Day, a Congregationalist. Early meetings of the Society were held in the Lyndhurst Hall, whose abandoned rear extension stands on your left (and which after 1973 housed the Camden Workers' Social Club for Council manual workers).

Considering Litcham Street properties to be beyond redemption, the SPHIS proposed replacing them with modern flats, each to have a bathroom and to be all-electric except for a coal-fired range. In April 1931 an appeal was launched to raise £100,000. Much of the fundraising took place in Hampstead, where 3,000 people attended a garden party held by Lady Pentland. A celebrity cricket match was played between a team of authors,

led by J B Priestley, and one of actresses, clad in beach pyjamas and captained by Gladys Cooper. Others playing included the writers Clifford Bax, A J Cronin, John Drinkwater, Louis Golding and Evelyn Waugh; and the thespians Flora Robson and Marie Ney.

The first stage of the Society's **Athlone Estate** was **Athlone House** (right), erected in 6 months and opened on 19 July 1933 by Princess Alice, Countess of Athlone. (The road became Athlone Street in 1937.) Three further blocks followed in an H formation: **Pentland House** (named after Lady Pentland) in 1936; the middle block, **Priestley House**, opened by the cricketing author and his wife Mary on 30 June 1937, and **Leonard Day House,** declared open on the same day, and named after a founder member who had died that year.

All four blocks were designed by the Society's regular architect, Ian Hamilton; but here there was none of the religious imagery commonplace on its Somers Town estates, and the buildings were named not after saints but after SPHIS supporters.

Several of these were alumnae of Sherborne School in Dorset. The Old Girls adopted the nursery school that was established on the roof of Priestley House, and which was named Sherborne Nursery School. Evacuated to Wiltshire during WWII, it returned to Kentish Town in 1945. ILEA assumed financial responsibility in 1973, and control later passed to Camden Council, until expenditure cuts forced the school's closure in the early 1990s. Resurrected, it now serves as the privately run **Rooftops Nursery**.

The SPHIS had hoped that Litcham Street would be closed entirely to enable more extensive redevelopment, but the authorities decided otherwise. So the north side, badly damaged in WWII, was redeveloped only in the 1960s. **Beckington** and **Ashington** are the southernmost blocks of the West Kentish Town Estate, with two more Somerset village names.

Pass under a low arched bridge beneath the North London Line. Cross Grafton Road and walk east along a short stretch of Holmes Road (see *Streets of Kentish Town*). At the crossroads by the George IV pub, turn left along **SPRING PLACE**. This was the earliest-developed street on this walk, in place by 1801 and originally a cul-de-sac off the end of what is now Holmes Road which, as Mansfield Place, had by 1796 struck west across the fields from today's 'High Street' (Kentish Town Road). Local springs, which gave Spring Place its name, fed the River Fleet, which flows southward, now underground, 100 metres east of here. They will also have supplied water to a brewery that once stood on the west side of the Place. The ratepayer there in 1845 was William

Holmes. Brewing was one sideline of the Holmes family, who owned and farmed much of the local land from a farmhouse off the high road to the east. Nearby, in Spring Place, was a 'rope ground', for the making of rope. The once semi-rural setting, with fine views towards the Northern Heights, was also an attractive place to live.

Early villas once lined much of the west side of Spring Place. Living here until his sudden death in 1805 was the printmaker James Parker, described by the sculptor Flaxman as an engraver "of distinguished merit" and "a punctual honest Man". In 1784 he had become a partner of the artist William Blake in a print-selling and publishing business and was Governor of the Society of Engravers. Another resident, until his wife's death (c.1841), was Henry Thomas Alken (1785-1851), the dominant sporting artist of the early 19th century, and a prolific creator of hunting, shooting, racing and coaching scenes. His biographer, W S Sparrow, wrote in 1927: "Out and about from his residence in Spring Place, Kentish Town, Henry Alken appeared quaintly countrified, oddly old fashioned ... His hat was ugly, low-crowned and broad-brimmed; his frock of Kendal green was dotted with large gilt buttons; and his gaiters and kickseys of brown cloth were in accord with a rustic waistcoat cut low, having ample pockets out of date but convenient for carrying

sketch-books. His shoes were thick and solid, and he preferred a walking staff to a walking stick."

Today a less rural scene would be hard to imagine. The Autograph Sound studio at **No.2** (left) occupies part of a site where Winsor & Newton established their first North London Colour Works, probably in a converted house. The world-renowned firm was founded in Rathbone Place [W1] in 1832 by William Winsor, an artist, and Henry C Newton, who provided the scientific expertise. In 1836 they invented Chinese White paint. Appointed artists' colourmen to Queen Victoria in 1841, they moved 3 years later to Spring Place, where colours were ground by hand, then spread out onto stone slabs for partial drying. The company later built a larger works farther along Spring Place. Its first factory at No.1 became a warehouse of Walton, Hassell & Port, listed as "Italian warehousemen" in 1874, and 90 years later still running a minor grocery chain with several branches locally (see pp 44, 61, 109).

The J T Coachworks (car bodywork) site at **Nos.3-5** has housed road transport enterprises for many years. London Lorries Ltd, "motor body builders", were here before WWII, after which the hauliers General Roadways took over the bomb-damaged site.

East of Spring Place lay Brick Field, where the Holmes family had diversified in the late 18th century from farming into the more lucrative business of brickmaking. The land was later purchased by the Midland Railway for its Kentish Town Coal Depot, which was fully operational by 1873. A prominent feature on old maps was the row of 16 raised red-brick arches, aligned east-west, that housed the depot's coal drops. There were 40 stables and coalmen's offices, within the depot site and facing Spring Place and Holmes Road. Coal operations ceased in c.1953, when the site became a British Road Services depot. Demolished in c.1972, this was replaced by the unattractive brick-and-concrete bulk of Camden Council's **Holmes Road Depot**, and the recycling depot off Spring Place (ahead).

Further along Spring Place, just past the railway bridge (a late-20th-century rebuild) the former works at **Nos.8-9** of the Eliott Optical Co. has given way to studios of the Wall to Wall TV company, producers of such historical 'reality dramas' as *The 1900 House*. In a similar line of business are the documentary makers October Films, winners of over 70 international awards, and among the present occupants of **Spring House** beyond. This was Winsor & Newton's second, purpose-built and steam-powered colour works, where they stayed until leaving for Wealdstone in 1938. Notice the upper-storey taking-in door and vestiges of hoists; note also the large windows, essential in an industry where natural light was at a premium.

Artificial light is manufactured here today, by Aktiva Lighting Systems, further tenants of the multiple-occupied building.

Opposite, recent yellow-brick housing stands on the site of commercial buildings served by Spring Sidings (Midland), which approached from the company's main line to the east.

The field beneath the sidings was Spring Meadow, farmed in 1806 by Richard Holmes 1806. He also rented the next meadow northward, the 4-acre 'Parish Field', one of the several 'Church Lands' in Kentish Town owned by St Pancras parish. It was traditionally accessed from Carker's Lane, off Highgate Road to the east, but became isolated from it when the Midland Railway line intervened.

On the Parish Field was built **ARCTIC STREET**, a short cul-de-sac on the right, originally named Franklin Street, probably after a builder. The LCC renamed it in 1937 by association with Sir John Franklin (1786-1847), the arctic explorer who disappeared with his ship and crew while searching for the North West Passage. A few old houses survive on the street's north side.

Walk on along **GILLIES STREET,** the later-built continuation of Spring Place. It was named after Margaret Gillies (1803-87), the miniaturist and watercolour painter, who lived in Fortess Road with her literary sister Mary and the sanitary reformer Dr Southwood Smith (see *Streets of Kentish Town*, p 136). On the near corner is **Carlton Chapel House**, with its unusual open staircase set within a trellised verandah. Designed in 1983-84 by Christopher Dean, it was built for the Tenants Association of North Camden (TANC) Housing Co-operative, as a plaque attests. Known since 2000 as the North Camden Housing Co-operative, the body continues to provide low-cost rented housing in the Kentish Town area. On this site, in one corner of the Parish Field, an iron church was erected in 1856 for the St Andrew's Mission District, forerunner of the church completed a decade later on Malden Road. The temporary church appears to have then been dismantled, as the site is shown as vacant on subsequent maps. By Edwardian times a new 'Carlton Hall', or 'Mission Hall' had appeared, similarly constructed in corrugated iron, but even more basic. The hall seems to have been both non-denominational and privately owned, the ratepayer Charles Pittman being recorded as its "proprietor". Around 1964 it assumed the name Carlton Chapel, which it kept until its closure in 1982.

Continue past the end of **WOODYARD CLOSE**, a modern L-shaped road whose northern end we encounter in Route 5 (p 98). Its southern arm, here on the right, once gave access to repair works where the Midland Railway maintained its road vehicle fleet.

Remaining in Gillies Street, continue to where it meets **QUEEN'S CRESCENT**. Here, to your right, is the small modern **Cresswood Hall** of the Grafton Area Residents Association, also home to the privately-run Cresswood Nursery (the name evidently concocted from Cressfield and Woodyard). This eastern end of Queen's Crescent was built in the 1850s as Cavendish Street. It suffered badly in the Blitz. Of its few original houses here, only **Nos.205-207** survive, on the right and approached by steep steps. A map of 1862 shows the roadway continuing eastward to Highgate Road, a scheme apparently abandoned when the Midland Railway cut across its route.

Reaching **GRAFTON ROAD,** note the pub on the corner opposite at No.149. Beginning life as the Manchester Tavern, it was soon renamed, in the wake of the Crimean War, as the **Mamelon Tower**. Taking its name from a French word for a woman's breast, the Mamelon was a Russian-held fortified hillock outside Sevastopol captured by the French and British allies in June 1855. An 'Irish' establishment in recent years, the pub was renamed the Man of Aran (alluding to the Aran Islands in Galway Bay), but in late 2005 reverted to its previous name.

Turn left and walk south. On your right is the eastern edge of the West Kentish Town Estate, and further 1960s low-rise blocks with Somerset village names:

Milverton, with **Wedmore** out of view behind, then Durston**,** and eventually Chelwood (both seen earlier).

This northerly section of Grafton Road was known until 1937 as Carlton Road. This 'estate agents' name', intended to lend the neighbourhood an air of gentility, was assigned in 1860, supplanting earlier individual terrace names. Although Victoria Terrace on the west side has been swept away, its companion, an identical Albert Terrace, remains opposite at **Nos.162-182**, a row of 3-storey houses with very small front gardens. Early residents included Rev. Owen Evans, an Independent minister, at No.178 (then No.75 Carlton Road) and at No.170 (then No.67) the wood engraver Josiah Copleston. Fellow printmaker Richard Austin Artlett (b.1807) died at the same address in 1873. Noted for his engravings of portraits and sculpture, he made 45 sculpture plates for the *Art Journal* in later life; several of his portrait engravings are in the British Museum. Artlett's five children were all baptised earlier in the century at St Pancras Old Church. No.73 (now No.176) was the address in 1904 of the Camden Brass Band of the London & North Western Railway; whether they rehearsed here is not recorded.

Beyond some post-WWII infill, **Nos.136-148** are the remnants of a once longer terrace, whose houses were arranged in twos, their front doors set back in

the joins between each pair. Here again the gardens are small – frustratingly so, perhaps, for the horticultural writer George M F Glenny, who lived at No.144 and whose *Gardening at a Glance* was published in 1879. In a vanished terrace opposite, No.28 Carlton Road was successively home to Isaac Henzel (1862-64) and T Roberts (1865-82), each a member of the Royal Society of British Artists. Now converted into flats, **No.73** on the corner of Warden Road was until recently the Carlton Tavern (note the surviving gilded lamp). This was once the local horse-bus terminus, from which omnibuses in orange or yellow livery departed for Victoria.

The opposite side of the road suffered severe bomb damage in the Blitz. Post-war commercial buildings erected here include new offices at **Nos.118-122**, sympathetically built in yellow brick with red trimmings on a site long occupied by the General Asphalte Co. Beyond Nos.104-108 is **Star House**, an uninspiring 1960s office-block, built on a site long occupied by Alfred & Co., makers of ice-cream refrigeration equipment. The block, which at first housed a quartet of metallurgical firms (such as Pinbrand Metals and Mitcham Smelters), has more recently been colonised by charities, latterly the Bergstern Foundation of the Jewish philanthropist Sir Sigmund Bergstern; the anti-racist Anne Frank Trust; the British Somali Community; and

Healthprom, founded in 1984 to promote health care in the then Soviet Union.

Crossing carefully to the west side, continue across Athlone Street (p 47) and pass under another low railway bridge. The printshop on the corner at **No.61**, dubbed the Athlone Press, is no relation to a namesake that was once the publishing house of London University. Walk on south to **East Fleet House** at No.55, a former chapel, built in 1867 for the Primitive Methodists and used by them until 1923 when they moved to Lamble Street (p 87). After their departure, the building was converted by St Pancras Council into an electricity substation. Serving more recently as a warehouse of the Abbey National Building Society, and then as offices, it was again refurbished in 2004. It is now home to Prelude Trading Ltd, a fashion supplier.

Grafton Road continues south to meet Prince of Wales Road. Developed here mostly in the 1850s, it ran along the eastern edge of Lord Southampton's estate, and took its name from the Duke of Grafton, then (as now) head of the Fitzroy family. (For that stretch of road, and all of the area south and east of this point, see *Streets of Kentish Town.*)

Turn right along **WILKIN STREET**. On your left, with barred ground-floor windows, is the grim north wall of an old piano factory. These were once the premises of John Brinsmead & Sons,

piano makers by royal appointment, of whose prestigious name the scam of 1896 (described on p 37) tried to take advantage.

Opposite, at **No.2**, is a small Victorian building occupied today by architects Walters & Cohen. Once the Primitive Methodists' Sunday School, it was hired by the London School Board in 1895 as a temporary school, until 1898 when its 200 pupils were transferred to the new Rhyl Street school (p 41). By contrast, and tucked in beside the North London Line viaduct at **No.3**, are the spanking-new glass-fronted offices of Eye Candy, website designers.

Next on the left, beyond yet another railway bridge, is the still cobbled cul-de-sac called **WILKIN STREET MEWS**. Numbered 55-66, the railway arches lining one side presumably derive their high numbers from their position along the whole length of the viaduct. Some are devoted today to car repair or bodywork. Cab proprietors were much in evidence here before WWI, when the street was known simply as Wilkin Mews. It was originally named Railway Arches. By 1868 arch No.1 had become the slaughterhouse of an aptly named John Death. Right next door at No.2 Railway Arches was the 'schoolhouse' of the Kentish Town Ragged School, later the Kentish Town Children's Mission of the Ragged School Union. Its volunteer teachers seem to have enjoyed the challenge of the spartan surroundings:

although the arch was enclosed at either end, decoration was minimal. Sunday school classes were still held here in the 1920s, partly thanks to Baptists from the Highgate Road chapel led by Detective Sergeant Morrish of Holmes Road Police Station. Mission activities were later transferred to the comparatively palatial Albert Hall (p 41).

Walk on along **WILKIN STREET**, passing on your left the new **Adventure Building** of the Talacre Play Centre (see below). The north side of the street is lined by the four blocks of the SPHA's **Athlone Estate**, which we viewed earlier (p 47).

Here, on either side of the railway viaduct, was the site of first St Pancras Almshouses **[14]**. The almshouse charity was founded in 1850 by Dr Donald Fraser and other local worthies. With the patronage of almost every major landowner in St Pancras parish, they raised £1,500 to buy a piece of land here from the Governesses' Institution (whose own 'Asylum' for retired governesses still stands in Prince of Wales Road, converted into luxury flats called The Gates, just east of this walk's starting-point). The almshouses, facing what became Wilkin Street, were designed by James Colling to house 100 people over 60. A central building, with a committee room and housing for two married couples, was flanked by two wings, each comprising nine houses accommodating four single inmates or

14   The first St Pancras Almshouses in what became Wilkin Street, c.1852

two couples. These almshouses were shortlived: after only four years, the HJR cut diagonally through their middle. The Court of Chancery ruled that the railway company need pay compensation only for the affected part of the building, a perverse decision later overturned on appeal. A new site was found in Southampton Road (p 75), where the present almshouses were opened in 1860. The surviving west wing of the original building, purchased by the HJR, became Nos.1-7 Railway Cottages. Their early occupants were a mixture of railway employees and manual workers in the building trade. Charles Booth, in 1898, commented on the Cottages' long front gardens, carved out of the almshouses' grounds. He coded the houses a 'fairly comfortable' pink, and likewise Stanmore Cottages immediately to the west, which he described as "new workers' flats, flush with the pavement". Both sets of Cottages survived until the building of the Athlone Estate, where Pentland House was opened on 29 April 1936 by Sir Josiah Stamp of the London, Midland & Scottish Railway, owners of the land as successors to the HJR.

Other land hereabouts was leased by Mary Jacomb [*sic*] Wilkin, a resident of Hampstead, where she ran a private high school for girls. At No.46 Wilkin Street, on the site of Athlone House, she opened a second establishment of more modest pretensions. Her 'Elementary & Middle Class Training School' was designed to attract the children "of respectable families, especially those who object to sending them to the Public schools". Its ethos was "thoroughly evangelical but undenominational"; so declared the school prospectus of 1874, which also bore the school motto: "Education is Systematic Training of the Hand, the Head and the Heart." By 1882 the establishment was listed as the Victoria Schools for Girls (Middle Class), with Miss Wilkin as "directoress". This was also the address of the Kentish Town Literary Institute, whose enthusiastic members presumably

met here at that time. By 1905, the by then redundant building was being used for worship by a group of Christian 'Brethren'. A year later it was taken over by the LCC, to serve until 1926 as a small junior mixed and infants school.

Almost opposite, in late-Victorian times, stood the Albert Lodge at No.47, to which the Good Templars had moved from Bassett Street (p 41), and which they shared with two like-minded bodies, the Haverstock Temperance Society and the Good Samaritan Total Abstinence Society.

Turn left into **Talacre Gardens** opposite, a welcome green lung of quite recent origin in this densely built-up district. Pause by a signboard bearing a useful potted history of the site, or find a nearby park bench on which to rest and digest its complex story. By 1849 terraced housing had already appeared along its west side in what is now Talacre Road (p 39), while the southern edge was lined by part of erstwhile Claremont Terrace facing what became Prince of Wales Road. The land behind Claremont Terrace remained open until the 1860s, serving a sporting purpose even then, as the Claremont Cricket Ground. By 1870, however, the site had been filled with working-class housing. Dickenson Street ran south from Wilkin Street before turning east to meet Dalby Street (see below). On the site of the present Quiet Garden, here in the northwest corner of the open space, was

a second, shorter L-shaped street, at first known as New Street but soon renamed Tovey Place. Building land here had been purchased by James Tovey Rowe, the landlord of the Cricketers (now Good Mixer) pub in Camden Town, whose shrewd investments allowed him to give up the pub and retire to a villa in Camden Road. William Henry Rowe, James's father and original partner in the enterprise, fared less well financially. He went bankrupt in 1861 and had to negotiate with one of his creditors, a Hertfordshire farmer called George Dickenson, hence the Dickenson Street name. Both streets were shaded purple (for 'mixed') on Charles Booth's later poverty map.

By 1894 an Anglican mission hall belonging to St Martin's (p 90) had opened near the northeast end of Dickenson Street, functioning there until WWI. On a previously undeveloped plot off the street's southeast corner, near the middle of the site, was built the Lister Works of R & J Beck Ltd, manufacturers of optical instruments.

Bomb damage locally during WWII, severest in the Tovey Place corner of the site, sowed the seeds of its gradual evolution into the present-day Gardens. The houses here were compulsorily purchased by the LCC in 1962, and progressively demolished. Local people formed the Talacre Action Group to promote play facilities for the young, and in August 1972 a play space was opened by Leslie Crowther, the children's TV presenter, where youngsters played against a backdrop of derelict war-torn houses. A fully equipped Adventure Playground was constructed more or less on the site of the present children's play area (ahead, left), though a 1973 plan to erect a 195-ft-high tower there, as a centrepiece, came to naught. An Adventure Room in a log cabin, opened in 1980, was the forerunner of today's **Adventure Building**, passed earlier. All remaining houses had been cleared from the site in 1979, and three years later the Talacre Open Space was complete, the old cricket ground restored to recreational use after a gap of over a century.

Sharing the Talacre site by then was Inter-Action, a group of charities and not-for-profit companies, founded in 1968 by the American actor Ed Berman OBE (b.1941). He later became special adviser on inner-city matters in the Conservative government's urban regeneration programme. The many projects which Inter-Action helped pioneer in the UK and Europe included community sculpture, city farms (see p 98), mobile arts and training facilities, community resource centres and youth and community telecommunication networks, and participatory children's theatre. The charity's own touring street theatre company, Prof. Dogg's Troupe, entertained with life-sized puppets.

A Community Arts Centre, designed by Cedric Price, was built over the north end of Dalby Street on the east side of the site. A 'no-frills' affair, steel-framed and with exposed girders and pipes, the centre was opened in 1977 by Princess Anne. Functioning there for a while was the Talacre Alternative School, an ILEA-funded establishment catering for truants from mainstream education. When in c.1987 Berman moved the HQ of his now sizeable charity to Docklands, changing its name to InterChange, the Talacre premises became InterChange Studios. Management training courses were held in the building, which also contained a resource centre and printshop serving voluntary organisations nationwide. Although intended to last for only 15 years, the centre featured in *The Buildings of England*, as "a rare demonstration of the Archigram vision of the high-tech plug-in city". When it was eventually pulled down, the massive debts incurred on it were controversially written off by Camden Council. (Still in Camden, the InterChange Studios now occupy the old Hampstead Town Hall on Haverstock Hill.)

In its place has arisen the Council's **Talacre Community Sports Centre**, built in 2001-02 at a cost of over £5 million, with a lottery grant from Sport England. Its facilities include a gymnastics training centre, a sports hall with 4 badminton courts, and an indoor soft play area for young children; and outside an artificial-turf pitch for football or hockey. Rebranded as Talacre Gardens, the Open Space has recently been refurbished.

Walking down the central footpath, turn left beyond the play area, to reach **DALBY STREET**. Now a cul-de-sac, this once continued north to meet Wilkin Street, lined by modest 2-storey houses and a few cheap shops, and with a Dalby Tavern on its west side. The street probably took its name from Mr Dalby, probably a sub-lessee of Miss Wilkin (p 53) and maybe one Jasper Boniston Dalby, who lived nearby at No.1 Queen's Terrace (p 66) and was recorded in the 1871 census as a "proprietor of houses". Opposite until late 2005, shoehorned between the street and the railway viaduct, was a neat collection of mobile homes, one of three official Camden Council caravan sites for 'Travellers'. The site is presently boarded up with corrugated iron.

Our own journey is now over. Kentish Town West station lies just around the corner at the end of the street.

Around St Silas
Circular walk from Chalk Farm station
For modern map see back cover

Silas, a companion of St Paul on his journeys, considered to have been the first bishop of Corinth, and said to have been martyred in Macedonia, is the unusual patron saint of a small Anglican parish that we traverse on this walk. To reach it, turn left on leaving Chalk Farm station, and cross straight ahead at the traffic lights to the northeast side of Chalk Farm Road.

Bear right and take the first turning left into **CROGSLAND ROAD**. This street was developed only in the late 1860s, well after most of the surrounding housing. It lies on land that was once the 3-acre Butchers Field, used in 1804 by Kentish Town farmer Richard Morgan. In 1818 Daniel Money leased the land as garden ground and set up Money's Nursery, taken over in the late 1830s by James Pearson, a Scottish seedsman and florist who ran it as the Eschol Nursery. Although one street map, in 1862, showed the garden as the 'Penrose Nursery', this was probably a mapmaker's error. Penrose *Cottage*, Hollis Cottage and a small Back Cottage, were three dwellings, erected during the Regency, that stood beside the nursery entrance, set back from the main road. The

five houses on the frontage there, northwest of Caroline Place (p 18) were known as Eschol Place. (The Grapes of Eschol, in the Old Testament, symbolise a land of plenty.) These houses had been developed from 1814 by Thomas Wheeler (p 68) and by Thomas Eaton, who in 1851, aged 93, was still living in Hollis Cottage. After Pearson's death in 1866, Crogsland Road was laid out over his nursery, and lined on both sides with terraced housing. The origin of the Crogsland street-name (approved in 1867) is a mystery since it does not appear to be a place-name or a surname. Perhaps the bend in the street suggested to someone with antiquarian interests that a name incorporating the Old English word for crooked (crog) would be apposite.

Likewise unknown is the derivation of Kirkwood Road, a cul-de-sac of modest houses built off the northwest side of Crogsland Road and leading eventually to the works at No.13 of T H Nott & Co, pianoforte action makers. Continue north past where the 1960s Crogsland Building of Haverstock School (p 69), which supplanted a war-damaged Kirkwood Road, was itself demolished in 2005 as part of the school's redevelopment. Walk on up Crogsland Road, passing on the right the columned rear of the Charlie Ratchford Centre (p 38) and one side of Denton flats (p 67) beyond. Opposite the latter is a surviving row of original houses at

Nos.1-11, renovated c.1983, where steep wide steps lead up to doorways arranged hall-to-hall.

In the 1870s Crogsland Road was home to the Assyriologist George Smith (1840-1876) who translated many cuneiform tablets − significantly, one containing a Babylonian account of the Flood. Smith's discovery suggested an alternative way of reading Genesis – as myth rather than history – and would be of profound significance to the entire field of Old Testament exegesis. The *Daily Telegraph* sponsored further Mesopotamian researches by Smith and in 1873 he found another fragment of the deluge story among the ruins of Assurbanipal's library at Kuyunjik. He conducted more expeditions, but contracted dysentery and died in the Middle East. In his time, no one in England had done more to bring the excitement and significance of archaeological discovery before the public.

A notorious interwar resident of Crogsland Road was a 42-year-old builder and decorator called Samuel Furnace. On 3 January 1933 a man was found burned to death in a builder's shed behind Hawley Crescent in Camden Town. A signed suicide note found nearby helped identify the dead man as Furnace. The conscientious St Pancras Coroner, William Bentley Purchase, was suspicious; he discovered that not only had the victim been shot, but he also had the teeth of a

ROUTE **3**

younger man, identified as Walter Spatchett, a rent collector aged 24. Furnace was found alive, and arrested. He admitted shooting Spatchett, but claimed it was accidental. It emerged that he had then faked his own suicide to cover his tracks, while allowing his wife to claim on the life assurance policy he had recently bought. Ironically, while in custody Furnace took a draught of hydrochloric acid from a bottle hidden in the lining of his overcoat, so making his suicide a reality.

Reaching Prince of Wales Road, carefully cross over and, veering left, turn right along **ST SILAS PLACE**. Known until 1937 as Palace Street, this was one of a pair of identical cul-de-sacs. Its companion, Crown Terrace, which was a little to the west, has now vanished. Although far from regal, their modest 2-storey terraces were described by Charles Booth in 1898 as "quite decent little places". Grade-II-Listed **St Silas the Martyr Church**, at the end of the Place, superseded an earlier mission church off Malden Road (see p 59) that was later the church hall. The new building was largely financed by a legacy from Howard Henry Paul, a wealthy American living in London. The foundation stone was laid on 16 December 1911 by Princess Marie Louise of Schleswig-Holstein (a granddaughter of Queen Victoria), who returned for the consecration of the church on 26 October 1912.

Built in purple-brown Fletton brick,

and in a Mediterranean Gothic style, the towerless church has an unusual arrangement of windows – a reminder that when it was built it was shut in on almost every side by 3-storey houses. St Silas was the first major commission of the architect Ernest Charles Shearman. The south porch and the Calvary outside, both also by Shearman, were unveiled in 1920 by the Bishop of Willesden in

remembrance of those killed in WWI. The figures in the corbels of the double porch are not "knights with armorial shields" (as English Heritage asserts) but Joan of Arc and St George; while the standing statue to the left is not of St Silas but of the Roman centurion who stood at the foot of the Cross. If you are lucky enough to gain entry, these riches are but a foretaste of the wealth of statuary within. There the

15 Members of the St Silas Players in 'The Mystery of the Passion' (courtesy St Silas the Martyr Church)

pinewood figure of St Silas depicts him standing on a reclining ox, and not being devoured by a lion (as is often the case). The church interior has narrow pointed arches, a narrow aisle, and a narrow gallery. The chancel, with a painted reredos by Victoria Somerville, has an open timber roof with neo-Gothic carvings.

Raised to parochial status soon after its opening, the new church became noted for its productions of Mystery Plays, specially written for the amateur St Silas Players [15] by Benjamin Boulter (a schoolmaster), with music by his wife Bertha. The Bishop of London forebade the performance of such plays in the church itself, and during WWI they took place in the church hall. When the diocese eventually relented in 1918, Boulter's Epiphany Play was the first Mystery to be staged in an English church since the Reformation. St Silas today remains faithful to the High Anglican ideals of its founder, Rev. G Napier Whittingham. One Ordnance Survey cartographer once mistakenly labelled it as an "RC Church", but C of E it is, and its parish is now combined with that of Holy Trinity, Hartland Road. Backtrack along St Silas Place where, after wartime bombing, the east side is lined by modern pale-brick flats named **Stonegate**.

Turn left along **PRINCE OF WALES ROAD**. Its north side here began as Dukesfield Terrace, named after the underlying field and presumably referring

to the Duke of Grafton, head of the Fitzroy family and relation of Lord Southampton. The solicitor's on the corner at **No.158**, once end-of-terrace and now free-standing, was a post-WWII rebuild of the Crown public house. Behind No.154 stood pre-war premises latterly occupied by the Hardware Brothers, motorcab proprietors; in the 1920s by a firm of carburettor makers; and before WWI by the London

THE FAMOUS MOTHER SHIPTON

Published as the Act directs by Samuel Baker Aug.t 1.1797.

16 Mother Shipton, 16th-century prophetess

Motor Coach Works. In earlier, horse-bus days, a yard here housed stables of the London General Omnibus Co. On the site today is **Shipton House**, a St Pancras Council block of 1951, which took its name from the pub beyond at the junction with **MALDEN ROAD**.

Renamed the **Fiddler's Elbow** in the 1990s, to the chagrin of many, this was previously the (Old) Mother Shipton. The eponymous lady, *alias* Ursula Sontheil, was the so-called 'Yorkshire Prophetess' [16], said to have been born in 1488 and (by some) to have lived at Knaresborough in a cave beside the River Nidd. (Others claim that she hailed from Norfolk.) Her alleged prophecies were published in Richard Head's *Life and Death of Mother Shipton* (1667), long after events whose dates she had supposedly prophesied, such as her own death and that of Cardinal Wolsey. Uncanny is the accuracy of the prediction that

Carriages without horses shall go.
And accidents fill the world with woe.
Around the world thoughts shall fly
In the twinkling of an eye…
Under water men shall walk,
Shall ride, shall sleep, shall talk;
In the air men shall be seen
In white, in black, and in green.
Iron in the water shall float
As easy as a wooden boat.

This verse first appeared in a 'reprint'

of Head's book in 1862 – well after the advent of ballooning, steam traction and iron ships, and four years after the laying of the first transatlantic telegraph cable! The 'prophecy' was added, as a hoax, by the book's publisher, Charles Hindley of the Strand. A further verse, of dubious authenticity, was of local interest:

> Before the good folk of this kingdom
> be undone
> Shall Highgate Hill stand in the midst
> of London.

The Malden Road pub, however, pre-dated Hindley's publication by several years. The Mother Shipton held a theatre licence in 1854-60. Now, as the Fiddler's, it is noted for its Sunday afternoon entertainment, usually Country music gigs.

With its corner in the form of a polygonal drum, the Grade-II-Listed pub occupies a focal position at a major crossroads, where our area's main east-west and north-south axes meet. This was also once an important tram stop. The London Street Tramways Co. laid its tracks along Malden Road in 1880. At first, all the horse-drawn trams running south to here from the Mansfield Hotel (p 104) turned left along Prince of Wales Road, heading for King's Cross and beyond via southeast Kentish Town. A further line along Malden Crescent and Ferdinand Street was authorised in the company's 1887 Act, and thereafter the Mother Shipton became a busy tramway junction. While some trams continued to follow the original route, others now continued straight ahead, running to Holborn or Euston via Camden Town.

Malden Road had been laid out by 1849, on the line of a footpath that once ran northwest towards the Gospel Oak across Hanging Ten Acres, actually a 16-acre field farmed in 1804 by Richard Morgan. The first six houses in Malden Road, built just north of the pub as Malden Terrace, are now replaced by 1960s council housing. All the road's earlier houses were terraced, not semi-detached as envisaged in suggested plans for the Southampton estate drawn up when it was sold off for building in 1840.

Cross over to the 1850s shopping parade opposite, originally named Newberry Place. This exemplifies the numerous changes in ownership and use undergone by local shops over time. **No.2**, on the corner, which began as an 'Italian warehouse', had by 1912 become a sub-post-office and from 1969 housed the Malden Road Neighbourhood Centre; later a video shop, it was boarded up in 2005. **No.4** served successively as another grocer's, then as coffee rooms and dining rooms, and later as an eel-pie shop; today it sells fish and chips.

No.10 was the Edwardian childhood home of Alfred Grosch, whose autobiographical *St Pancras Pavements* was published in 1947. He grew up over the corn and seed shop managed here by his father William, who (he wrote) always wore a white apron and alpaca jacket when serving customers. Alfred had fond memories of his shopkeeping neighbours: the "bearded and most gentlemanly tea grocer" at No.2, presumably and at **No.14**, "a quaint old chap [Edward Antoni]" who made umbrellas. **No.22** was an oil and colour shop of the once ubiquitous Joseph Salmon chain; "its chief assets", wrote Grosch, "were two pretty and vivacious daughters". He was less complimentary about the local populace at large, whom he described as "brutal and pugnacious" and spending money on drink, while their "barefoot, hungry children, clad in rags … raked over the refuse heaps in Queen's Crescent in search of half rotten fruit".

Among Alfred's immediate neighbours were the "not always savoury or sober Mews' dwellers". These were the inhabitants of **NEWBURY MEWS**, still accessed today through a covered entry beside No.10. It began as Newberry Mews. Thomas Weeding, the nephew of Thomas Weeding Senior (d.1856), owner and developer of land eastward, inherited the estate, but he soon died, in 1864, leaving a pregnant wife Elizabeth, née Newberry. Their son, named Thomas Newberry Weeding, died aged only 18 months, and the estate passed to another great-nephew of Thomas Weeding Senior, Thomas Weeding Bagallay. He, incidentally, was obliged under the terms of his benefactor's will to change his surname by royal licence to Weeding, so becoming Thomas Weeding Weeding. But it was his deceased infant relation's middle name that lived on here. (Although, coincidentally, both the Weedings and Lord Southampton's Fitzroy family owned land in the Surrey parish of Malden, it was probably the Fitzroy connection that inspired the naming of Malden Road.)

Costermongers once found a home in Newbury Mews and parked their barrows there. In 1914 the only listed businesses were a blacksmith and a firewood dealer. As late as 1926, a horseflesh dealer, Harry Bradbury, was recorded at No.1. The mews had been coded dark blue ('very poor') by Charles Booth. While spotting "no brothels" here in 1898, he considered it "a hole and corner sort of place that ought to be cleared out". His wish was fulfilled a century later, when the mews was redeveloped by Keith Meehan of Lincoln Holdings (winners of RIBA awards for other, more prestigious projects such as Islington's Gainsborough Studios). In Newbury Mews they built 13 very small houses intended for the 'dinky' market (dual income, no kids yet). When buyers failed to materialise, the developers were forced to turn landlord and rent out the properties instead. To protect residents' privacy in the very narrow mews, much use is made here of frosted glass. Modern block paving strives to imitate the original cobbles.

Former Newberry Place continues north past **ST LEONARD'S SQUARE**, at the entrance to which we pause. This is not a square at all, but a wide cul-de-sac of square-cut 3-storey houses. At its dead end no fewer than five houses face west, the front gardens on each flank angled to fit the available space. A map of 1849 suggests that this was to have been a through route to Weedington Street (now Talacre Road), but the way was later barred by house-building on the latter's west side (p 39). The derivation of the St Leonard's name is unknown. Bebbington's speculation that both Square and Mews took their names from places in Kent loses credibility if Newberry, as noted above, had a family origin. Despite its pretentious name, the Square was largely working-class from the outset. On his 1889 poverty map, Booth shaded it a 'poor' light blue. A decade later he thought it a "roomy spot, rather rough at times; but [with] a mixed up set of people living in it". He "saw several tidy and clean children, and some of the houses spick and span", sufficiently so to earn a coding upgrade to purple.

If 1960s planners had had their way, neither Square nor Mews would exist today. The whole rectangular block eastward to Talacre Road would have been cleared, to become the western half of an open space almost twice the size of today's Talacre Gardens (p 53). **MALDEN ROAD** would have been skewed to the east here at its south end, to make way for a pedestrian square, adjoining the council flats that were built on the west side. Find a gap in the traffic to cross carefully back to that side of the road, here lined by one side of the **St Silas Street South Estate**. This we shall briefly penetrate, following the footway beside the modern shops on the north side of 6-storey **Leysdown**. Note at **No.11** the Congolese Action Group, which provides drop-in advice and information services for Congolese students and refugees and asylum seekers from Angola and Congo Brazzaville.

The pathway corresponds to former Shipton Place, an impasse named Whitefield Street until 1886, maybe after the 18th-century evangelist George Whitefield, said by some (on no firm evidence) to have preached beneath the Gospel Oak tree. Ahead is the former St Silas (Mission) Hall. In 1877 Rev. M J Sutton was appointed missionary to the new St Silas Mission District established by the London Diocesan Mission. Early activities were held at first out of doors, and then in local houses. After five years, Rev. P R Malony began planning for a new mission church. Bear right and turn left past its foundation stone, laid in May 1884 by Lady Wilfreda Biddulph. Designed in an Early English style by C L Luck, the mission church had 150 seats to serve a District population of 5,566. Ritualistic services introduced by Rev. F W Bentley in 1892 were continued by the strongly Anglo-Catholic Rev. Napier Whittingham when he took over as priest-in-charge in 1907. Five years later, the mission became the church hall of the newly built St Silas. Follow the latter's north wall westward to view its disused north porch, where the six empty niches were meant to house statues that were never added.

You are now in what was once Preston Street, a narrow L-shaped street of 3-storey houses that ran west off Malden Road before turning north to meet Marsden Street. When Charles Booth walked the area in 1898 with Inspector Tomkin, he classified it dark blue (for very poor). It was, he wrote, "described by Tomkin as 'as bad as possible' and clearly reckoned by him as the worst spot in this sub-division". There were, the policeman said, "a good many thieves and prostitutes. The thieves are not experts, but it is an ugly place, not safe at night". With both a right-angled turn and a curve at its west end, it was hard to police, "not easily commanded from either end". Booth further noted "a mission room with bespattered, rarely used door and closely wired windows seemed to show that the street regarded it as an intruder".

Preston Street became St Silas Street in 1913, soon after the opening of the church, and remained as such until swept away in the building of the St Silas Street Estate. This comprehensive redevelopment, designed for Camden Council by G B Drewitt, and completed in 1966, comprises several pale-brick blocks of modest height, ranged along surrounding roads and around a central play area (right). Each block is named after a village in Kent.

Return eastward, noting as you go the slight angle in the frontage between church and church hall, corresponding to the very bend in Preston Street of which Tomkin complained. Veer left to re-emerge into Malden Road through a triple-arched exit beneath 6-storey **Headcorn**. Turn left and continue north to the next crossroads. On its southeast corner stood the Newberry Arms pub, which at one time became the Newbury Arms but later reverted to its proper name, surviving until controversially demolished in 2005.

Intersecting here is **MARSDEN STREET**, shown as laid out but undeveloped on a map of 1849. The terraced housing that was soon to appear formed four separately named terraces. To your left, Prince's (or New Prince's) Terrace on the north side faced a Marsden Terrace on the south. Thomas Marsden was a wholesale druggist in the City who invested his money in Kentish Town land. East of the crossroads, the two sides of the street were respectively named Durnford Place and Durnford Terrace, Durnford being a Wiltshire village name. By 1870 the whole length of the street had become Durnford Road, remaining thus until 1886 when it assumed its present name.

Charles Booth, in 1898, described the west end of Marsden Street as "very respectable and decent looking". Today the light-brick **Burmarsh** block of 1966 lines the south side of the street, with **Chislet** flats beyond. Units in Burmarsh Workshops are let by Camden Council to small businesses, in fields such as antique restoring and photography. On the street's north side is one arm of L-shaped brown-brick Southfleet (see later).

Crossing Malden Road, stroll part way along Marsden Street's eastern end. On the left is the playground of Rhyl Primary School (p 41), whose twin spires (not easily seen from Route 2) are now clearly visible. Old houses remain beyond at **Nos.10-22**, 2½-storey with steps up to their front doors. Opposite, a complete 3-storey 1850s terrace survives at **Nos.1-49**. Some houses retain their iron balconettes; note particularly the fine bulbous examples on **No.19**. This eastern part of Marsden Street rated only purple ('mixed') shading on Booth's poverty map. **No.37**, in April 1973, was the scene of an incident headlined by the press as the 'Marsden Street Siege'. Squatters facing eviction had barricaded themselves inside. Taking the law into their own hands, frustrated local residents stormed the house, summarily ejecting the squatters, one of whom suffered minor injuries when he fell while running away. Jock Stallard, the local MP, referred in the Commons to this "eruption of violence", which he blamed on the housing shortage.

Return to **MALDEN ROAD**, past diminutive single-storey **No.42A** (facing Marsden Street), in Edwardian times the GP's surgery of Dr William Duke Gorges Mulloy. Turn right, past **Nos.42-58**. Dating from the 1850s, and originally known as Upper Newberry Place, this further range of shops was the last terrace to be built in the piecemeal development of this end of Malden Road. Five of the shopfronts are now disused. Before WWI, No.44 housed the Kentish Town branch of the British Socialist Party. At Nos.50-52, now part occupied by the Kentish Town Dental Centre, was the longstanding pawnbroking business of Long & Doughty (later John Long Ltd). At No.54 Harry Griggs' Edwardian eel-pie house had been replaced after WWII by a shop selling Jaylex ladies' handbags. The corner shop and off-licence beyond, at No.58, which in 1907 was a branch of the local grocery chain of Walton, Hassell & Port, later became a second-hand furniture shop.

Across Rhyl Street (p 40), on the site of modern **No.60**, another sometime pawnbroker's shop was invaded in 1972 by an anarchic group of squatters, led by one 'Donegal Joe' McGarrigle and adopting such outlandish names as the Free High

Church, the Digger Action Movement and the White Panther Party. The empty building they dubbed The Polytantric, opening there a short-lived 'free shop' and offering meditation and judo lessons.

This junction was once a staggered crossroads, where Rhyl Street continued west (to your left). There, in 1886, it had absorbed an earlier-built and narrower Duke's Terrace. Booth later found this now vanished end of Rhyl Street to be "improved and quiet".

Opposite today is the long 6-storey block named **Southfleet** (after another Kentish village), part of the **St Silas Street North Estate** built by Camden Council in 1969-75 as a continuation of the redevelopment begun earlier to the south. Designed by the Council's own architects, and characterised by brown-brick construction with long projecting balconies, the estate is described in Cherry & Pevsner as "a forbiddingly dense craggy group". In the terrace of shops that Southfleet supplanted, No.43 served from 1946 as the West Kentish Town Library. Public library provision had always been a low priority for St Pancras Borough Council, and it was not until after WWII that this area gained its first. Even then it wasn't purpose-built, but converted from a former house and bootmaker's shop. The 'temporary' library **[17]** remained in use for some 21 years until replaced by Camden's new, but also temporary,

Athlone Street building (p 47).

The former row of shops began as Ponsford Terrace; James Ponsford was a West London builder, who owned a wharf in Paddington Basin. Having built much of Bayswater and Tyburnia, and collaborated with Thomas Cubitt in Belgravia, he was listed by 1845 as an 'architect'. Unscathed by allegations that he had defrauded house-buyers, James continued building, in northern suburbs such as St John's Wood and Kentish Town. By 1861 he was a wealthy man, the owner of a Mill Hill mansion and employer of a dozen servants. At No.9 Ponsford Terrace (later No.55 Malden Road) was the Ponsford Arms public house. Living at No.8, and dying there in 1859, was Thomas Kibble Hervey, the poet and journalist who, as editor of *The Athenaeum*, had campaigned for such humanitarian causes as prison reform. His wife Eleanora (née Montagu) was an established poet in her own right and, after her husband's death, published a 3-volume novel, *Snooded Jessaline, or the Honour of a House*.

Walk on up the east side of Malden Road as far as **No.74**, opposite which a now vanished Modbury Street once ran westward across the Southfleet site. Kinsmen of James Ponsford, likewise active in West London as architects or builders, had hailed from the South Devon village of Modbury. Coding Modbury Street a 'quite comfortable' pink in 1898,

Booth singled out one poorer dwelling, "tucked away at N side of E end, a wood-chopper's queer crib, quite different to anything else in the street". On its south side, by Edwardian times, stood the mission hall of St Andrew's Church (p 94), soon to be renamed the St Andrew's Hall and Institute. The St Andrew's Institution (*sic*) for Youths and Men had first opened in 1874 in the National Schools (p 96). It catered for both educational and recreational needs: games played in its early days included not only chess, draughts and dominoes, but also 'German Tactics'. In 1921 a marble tablet was erected on the north wall of the parent church in memory of parishioners who had given their lives in WWI. The inscribed roll of honour was headed: "Old Modburian Club, Forward Modbury, 1914-1918". Later, after WWII, the Modbury Street hall housed the Thanet Boy's Club. Occupying a triangular site off the north side of the street was a 3-sided Modbury Mews (later Modbury Yard); **Fordcombe** flats now cover much of its site.

Continue past **Nos.70-104** on the right, a 3-storey 1850s terrace that formed the northern half of Upper Newberry Place. Here the basement areas are protected by spearhead railings, while many of the ground-floor window ledges still bear their original unusual iron window-box supports. By 1864 several of the houses had been colonised by private schools. A school for young gentlemen at No.76, run by J T Drawbridge, adjoined Mrs Emily Lawrence's ladies' school at No.78. Next door at No.80 was a 'commercial and collegiate school' run by William Temple, MCP (Member of the College of Preceptors). A decade later, it was superseded by John Barter's grandiosely named Malden College, while at adjacent No.82 *George* Temple's 1860s ladies' school had given way to one run by Mrs Ffarmer.

A display entry in the 1864 directory proclaimed **No.102** as the address of Bedford & Morgan, an obscure and seemingly short-lived firm of harmonium makers. Still trading on the corner beyond, and retaining its original name, is the **Sir Robert Peel** pub. The eponymous

17 The 'temporary' library at No.43 Malden Road, which functioned for 21 years

Tory statesman, twice prime minister and best remembered for establishing the 'Peelers' and 'Bobbies' of the Metropolitan Police, had died in 1850 shortly before the pub opened. One wonders how the local Irish community reacted to the name: Sir Robert, as Irish Secretary, had been strongly anti-catholic, earning himself the nickname 'Orange Peel'.

Opposite is **Cheriton,** the northernmost block of the St Silas Street North Estate, fronted by an arrow-shaped parade of modern shops, now largely abandoned. At Nos.27-30 Cheriton is the **CarAf Centre** of the Camden Black Parents and Teachers Association. Founded in 1980, this had led a nomadic existence in temporary premises before settling here. Its facilities include the Mandela (originally Winnie Mandela) Supplementary School. Cross over to admire the colourful mosaic mural on the Queen's Crescent corner. The images were chosen by nine young people to reflect their experiences on a youth project 'Heritage Trip' to the Gambia in October 2002. The design represents "the tree of life from daytime to night-time", hence its two halves, in red and orange and in purple and blue.

Cross **QUEEN'S CRESCENT**, where **No.129** on the corner, now strangled by ivy, was as Priory House once home to a Victorian surgeon. It later became a St Pancras Council Maternity &

Child Welfare Centre, and served after WWII as a Welfare Centre of the LCC. **No.127**, next door to the left, was home in the late 1970s to Joseph Gorman-Sickert, who claimed to be the son of the officially childless painter, Walter Sickert. Stories supposedly told to him by his alleged father before his death in 1942, implicating the Victorian Royal Family in the Whitechapel Murders of 1888, formed the basis of Stephen Knight's book, *Jack the Ripper, the Final Solution* (1976). Joseph was subsequently interviewed by Special Branch. Nos.127&129 and the houses to their left were initially part of Queen's Road Villas. These continued round the corner into Malden Road, embracing the short terrace beyond No.129 at the present **Nos.99-105 Malden Road**.

Continue briefly north past these, and then turn left into **HERBERT STREET**. This Y-shaped street was a combination of two short cul-de-sacs that eventually met at an acute angle. This northern arm began as Queen Street. House-building here, late infill, was still incomplete in 1870. Later shaded by Charles Booth in a 'fairly comfortable' pink, most of the modest houses built are still intact. Up on the right, on the end wall of No.31, is an old painted sign that identified the now extinguished Chaston Street (p 79). New grey-panelled housing beyond at No.29 covers the site of an Edwardian laundry, and a beershop at No.29A that survived

until WWII. In the top right-hand corner of the street, a footpath leads through to Thurlow Terrace (p 79). We, though, turn sharp left down the original Herbert Street, which was named after Vincent Herbert, a Hoxton-based builder.

In the angle between the street's two arms stands the Victorian **Malden Hall**, with its pattern of round-headed windows and red brick banding on the walls, long home to the non-denominational Evangelistic Mission. In March 1880, at a Tramway Navvies' Evening, 200 men laying tramlines in Malden Road were treated here to a lavish tea, followed by gospel-hymns sung by the 'open-air band' and a sermon by a repentant bricklayer. The following February, a meeting arranged by Mr Stidolph of the mission was attended by 400 unemployed men, many of whom will have lost their jobs in that bitterly cold winter. A "coloured preacher" was among the attractions. After many years in Herbert Street, the mission had moved by 1960 to the redundant Parkhill Chapel in Fleet Road (Hampstead). Malden Hall has since served young people in various ways. In 1975 it housed a juvenile crime attendance centre, where convicted soccer hooligans were given gym lessons, played football and learned a craft. By 1978 the Hall was playing host to an erstwhile Thanet Play Group. Right of the doorway, a mosaic wall-plaque, bearing the initials "CYWC", recalls the Camden Young Women's Centre that, with Council funding, flourished here for a while from 1979. Still going strong is the Thanet Youth Club, successor to the boy's club previously in vanished Modbury Street. In 2005 it merged with the Goal Youth Club as part of the Ashdown Youth Project.

Lower down on the left at **No.2** is a sheltered hostel of 1991-93 by Avanti Architects on the site of a small yard used in 1907 by the builder Alfred Henry Tout, and still half a century later by the Tout family firm.

Regain **QUEEN'S CRESCENT** part way along its south-western section. Here the underlying land was once Blue Barn Field, an 18-acre meadow rented in 1804 by Thomas Rhodes, who farmed countless acres throughout St Pancras parish and who was an ancestor of the colonialist Cecil Rhodes. By 1835 the ground here had become a nursery. Built up from the earlier 1850s, the present part of the Crescent was called Queen's Road until 1863 (Victoria was the honoured queen). It has always been quite different in character from the later-developed 'market' stretch (p 42) to your left, whose entrance is announced by the prominent sign above the road. Quiet and residential, it was long known by locals as the 'Private End'. Its dignified 3-storey houses were originally the family homes of middle-class professionals and businessmen. By 1900 many of them had

been converted into apartments.

Nos.115-129, to your left, were at first part of Queen's Road Villas, encountered earlier. One resident of No.117 was Frederick Augustus Whitehead, an Edwardian manufacturer of false teeth. The opposite side, now lined by further flats of the St Silas Street North Estate, was once a terrace of houses, and a sprinkling of shops, facing straight onto the pavement. Here No.54 was home in 1863-66 to the artist Arthur Boyd Houghton. He moved here (from Richmond) to be nearer to the Dalziel Brothers, the Camden Town engravers and publishers, for whom he produced much work and who became his close friends. Houghton's evocative depictions of London life included the well-known street scene entitled *Holborn 1861*. After his wife Susan died of pyaemia on the birth of their third child, the artist moved to King Henry's Road (Hampstead), where he eventually drank himself to death, aged 39.

Turn right. The next forty houses southward on the right were all originally numbered as part of a long Queen's Terrace, although the variety of styles suggests piecemeal development by several different builders. Notice the bold, eccentric porticoes at **Nos.105&107**. Living at **No.101** in 1981 was Frank Delaney, the Irish novelist and BBC broadcaster, who created Radio 4's

language programme *Word of Mouth*.

ST THOMAS' GARDENS (next right) is the first of four delightful cul-de-sacs off the west side of Queen's Crescent, built in the 1850s, probably by Vincent Herbert (see Herbert Street, p 63). Booth described them as "all of the same character, 2½-st[orey], quiet and respectable". His assessment is equally true today. Each road climbs steadily to end abruptly at the boundary of the Maitland Park estate (p 72). Some original Windsor-style street lamps survive, albeit no longer lit by gas. The stuccoed houses are all individually painted in different pastel colours. Although two of the cul-de-sacs have been renamed, all four once bore the names of Christian saints. Victorian developers would sometimes name streets after people connected with them, then 'sanctify' them, not out of piety but as an attraction to buyers.

With low-rise **Halstow** flats to your left, pass **No.99 Queen's Crescent** opposite, home in 1973 to Elkan Allan and wife Angela, co-authors of a guide to televised movies that was published that year. Elkan, who a decade earlier had created the seminal ITV pop-music show *Ready, Steady, Go*, went on to become a journalist and writer on poker.

Walk on to the second cul-de-sac. Previously known as St John's Gardens, this became **BAPTIST GARDENS** in 1937, the new name derived not from the nonconformist denomination but from St John the Baptist. **Lenham** flats line the east side of the Crescent as we continue past **No.71 Queen's Crescent**, to which Mr Drawbridge moved the gentlemen's school encountered earlier in Malden Road.

Crossing **ST ANN'S GARDENS**, which still bears its original name, walk on along **QUEEN'S CRESCENT**, noting the continuous iron balcony at **Nos.47-59**. Living in 1867 at No.59 was Lionel Charles ('Bill') Henley, a genre painter and exhibiting member of the Society of British Artists for some 30 years.

Opposite on the next left-hand corner, at **No.2**, stands the former Queen's Arms, sole survivor of the 1850s east-side terrace. A later side-extension, facing Marsden Street, bears the inscription "1896". The hostelry has been rebranded in recent years as the **Monkey Chews** pub-restaurant, its name a Northern slang term for 'drunk'.

South of Marsden Street is the site of the Tailors' Almshouses **[18]**. The Benevolent Institution for the Relief of Aged & Infirm Journeyman Tailors was established in 1837, perhaps partly in response to a recent tailors' strike, and initially occupying two houses in Pimlico. The first stone on the Kentish Town site was laid in May 1842 by the Marquis of Salisbury. Set in 1½ acres of garden, four of the almshouses were built by

subscription, the other six by John Stulz, a prosperous West End tailor. He also endowed the central chapel, dedicated to St John the Evangelist, and consecrated by Bishop Blomfield in June 1843. A

18 The Tailors' Almshouses c.1904; note the lady cyclist

parsonage housed a resident chaplain, the Rev.Thomas Appleby. By the 20th century the chaplain's managerial role had passed to a matron, and pastoral care was provided by the curate of St Silas, who encouraged the general public to worship at "St John's". The Institution was founded "for the support of aged tailors of every nation in the world irrespective of creed". Early census returns list some 65 inmates, all retired tailors (or their wives), and including many octogenarians. They hailed from every corner of the British Isles, but despite the ambitious mission statement,

the most far-flung birthplace recorded was Ireland. High maintenance costs led

the charity to relocate in 1937, to a new Nursing & Rest Home at Shirley, South Croydon. The Queen's Crescent site was sold to St Pancras Borough Council.

Upon it was erected the present rambling block of council flats in red and grey brick, originally named Montague Tibbles House in honour of Henry Montague Tibbles JP, a St Pancras councillor and Guardian of the Poor who had died in 1937. Arranged symmetrically around a central space, the flats bear all the hallmarks of A J Thomas, the conservative architect of much of St Pancras Council's interwar housing.

Including the 1000th flat to be built by the borough, the block opened in 1939 on the eve of WWII, only to become a victim of the Blitz, hit by a mine on the night of 16 April 1941; sixteen people lost their lives. By the late 1960s the poor conditions here, described as "near-slum", prompted a complete refurbishment of the flats. They were also renamed **Penshurst**, which Kentish name brought them into line with their post-war neighbours. Living in Flat 102 in the 1970s, with his wife Teresa, was the versatile musician John Chilton (b.1932), jazz trumpeter and flugelhorn player, composer and arranger, jazz historian, and leader of the Feetwarmers band that often backed George Melly.

Opposite Penshurst is the last of the four cul-de-sacs, known as St James's Gardens until 1937 when, perhaps to avoid confusion with the disused burial ground near Euston, it became **MODBURY GARDENS**, borrowing its new name from the then still extant Modbury Street (p 61). Early residents of the cul-de-sacs were typically lower middle-class – widows of professionals or clerks in the civil service, in business or on the railways. **No.4**, in 1861, housed a surgeon's widow and her son, a clerk at the Post Office Directory; while a "clerk to the Danish consulate" lived at **No.6** with his sister, a "money taker at Madame Tussaud's".

Beyond, in **QUEEN'S CRESCENT,** observe the castellated bay windows at **Nos.39-43**, which also boast pierced parapets. No.1 Queen's Terrace, now **No.37**, was once home to Jasper Boniston Dalby, the landlord after whom Dalby Street (p 54) may well have been named. Here the long Queen's Terrace ended: **Nos.33&35** were initially Nos.1&2 Modena Terrace. All the houses south of No.31 have been replaced by modern flats. Vanished No.25 Queen's Crescent was still a ladies' school in 1914, run by Mrs Elizabeth and Misses Grace & Ellen Watson. That year saw the death at No.21 of the bibliophile Bertram Dobell. Born in Sussex in 1842, he endured an impoverished childhood as the son of a journeyman tailor who became paralysed and fell on hard times. Aged about 30, Bertram sank his meagre savings (and a £10 advance from a loan society) into opening a bookshop-cum-stationer's at No.62 Queen's Crescent (p 42); just £3 was spent on book stock. The workaholic Dobell went on to become a respected literary scholar and the owner of two bookshops in Charing Cross Road. The journalist Lewis Doxat died at No.13 in 1871, having served for many years as manager of *The Observer*. Living next door at No.11 was the landscape painter John Syer (1815-1885), a founder member of the Royal Society of British Artists.

Other Queen's Crescent residents have included the actor Jonathan Pryce (c.1986), and fifty years earlier the communist writer Randall Swingler. Also a poet and flautist, Swingler had married the concert pianist Geraldine Peppin in 1933. The next year they joined the Communist Party, to which Randall donated all of the fortune inherited from his father, a wealthy Midlands ironmaster and coalmine owner.

The flats of Silverbirch Walk are officially in Maitland Park Road (see p 83), round the next right-hand corner, which was once lined by terrace houses known as Albert Villas. We rejoin **PRINCE OF WALES ROAD** at its western end. Ever broad and tree-lined, this section was at first briefly known as Prince of Wales Avenue. Rebuilt **No.200**, not quite opposite, stands on part of the site of the Bedford Nursery (p 69). Cross over carefully and turn left along the south side, past the 3-storey terrace at **Nos.181-199**, noting the segmental pediments above many of the first-floor windows. Behind **No.179**, before WWII, were workshops owned by John Smith Tozer, a coverer of pianoforte hammers. The houses at **Nos.169-179** have a continuous first-floor balcony with fretwork supports.

CRADDOCK STREET on the right, at present unnamed, is a short cul-de-sac once lined by terrace housing, which took its name from William Craddock, a bootmaker of Moreton Terrace (Kentish Town Road) who leased land here c.1860 when the street was built. In the wake of wartime bombing, No.4 was labelled as a "ruin" on a post-WWII map, and along with its neighbours was later pulled down. Long bereft of its houses, the street was freshly resurfaced in 2005, though it leads only to the perimeter fence of the Haverstock School building site and serves only as a car-park. Craddock Street and Truro Street (see below) previously served as the two main entrances to the school, which had only footpath access from Haverstock Hill.

On the north side of **PRINCE OF WALES ROAD** stands the former Methodist church, built for the Wesleyan congregation that had previously worshipped in Bassett Street (p 41). Visible behind is the "school-chapel" that was built first, set back from the road, in 1867 and which later became the Sunday School. In front of it, four years later, an imposing church arose, its classical 5-bay pedimented portico, faced in Bath stone, boasting two gigantic Composite columns. The galleried interior offered seating for 1,050. The church thrived, becoming the head of a new Prince of Wales 'Circuit' in 1904. Mounting maintenance costs forced the church's closure in the 1960s, its congregation merging with the Gospel Oak Methodists in Agincourt Road.

The redundant building was soon occupied by Drama Centre London, founded in 1963 by a visionary group of tutors and students – "prospective actors and actresses who were willing to help raise money and to put up with almost any conditions in order to be trained in a particular way". That "way" was Method Acting. The Centre was a training-ground for several world-famous directors, and numerous well-known actors, including Pierce Brosnan, Simon Callow, Frances de la Tour, Colin Firth, Tara Fitzgerald, Anastasia Hille, Geraldine James and Penelope Wilton. The Drama Centre has now moved to Holborn as part of the Central Saint Martin's College of Art and Design. The Grade-II-Listed former church awaits a buyer for its "valuable freehold".

Once lined by shops, Prince of Wales Road east of the church now borders further low-rise flats of the 1960s St Silas Street Estate. The former Crown Terrace (see p 56) leads to **Otterden**. Next to the east is **Wingham**, with **Westwell** tucked away behind. Each block bears a predictably Kentish place-name.

Unexplained is the name of **TRURO STREET**, opposite. This cul-de-sac was a virtual twin of Craddock Street and has suffered a similar fate, all of its terraced housing long gone. Erstwhile No.9 was home in 1861 to Edward Albert Foley (1814-74), the Dublin-born sculptor, elder brother of the better-known John Henry Foley, and a specialist in busts. Rev. David Laing, vicar of nearby Holy Trinity, was among his subjects.

In **PRINCE OF WALES ROAD**, on either side of Truro Street, is the surviving western half of Roxburgh Terrace (p 38). Some of the houses west of Truro Street sport an ornate cast-iron balcony running conventionally at first-floor level. Eastward, at **Nos.131-149**, the ground floor too is similarly embellished. Metal pillars link the two levels, producing an unusual colonnade effect that has earned the terrace a mention in *The Buildings of England*. It is, however, the same effect that we witnessed earlier (p 66) at Nos.169-179.

Living at No.141 in October 1890 was Phoebe Hogg, the wife of furniture remover, Frank. He had a mistress, known as 'Mrs Mary Pearcey', although actually a Miss Wheeler. The 24-year-old daughter of a convicted murderer, Mary lived in Priory (now Ivor) Street in southeast Kentish Town. Perhaps jealous of her newborn baby, Mary invited Phoebe to tea, reportedly spying from the corner of Crogsland Road (ahead) while a messenger boy delivered the invitation to No.141. Mrs Hogg promptly went with her child to Priory Street for tea. An argument ensued, after which Phoebe lay dead, badly battered and with her throat cut. Draping her victim's body across the baby's pram, and thus suffocating the child, Mary set off with the pram on a 6-mile walk through the streets. Phoebe's corpse she dumped in Crossfield Road (Swiss Cottage); the baby's she left in a field beside Finchley Road; and the pram, which eventually

19 Mary Pearcey in the dock at Marylebone Police Court (Daily Graphic, 28 Oct 1890)

collapsed, she abandoned off Maida Vale. There was no shortage of witnesses. Mary was subsequently arrested, tried for murder **[19]** and (like her father before her) hanged.

On our own shorter perambulation, we have come full circle. Retrace your earlier steps down Crogsland Road (right), with the Roundhouse prominent in the distance, to return to Chalk Farm station for your transport home.

Route 4
Through Maitland Park
Circular walk from Chalk Farm station
For modern map see back cover

This walk explores the frontier territory of Maitland Park and its western boundary with Hampstead, and includes the site of the Gospel Oak. We begin and end at Chalk Farm Tube station on the Northern Line at the foot of Haverstock Hill, the ancient southern approach to Hampstead.

Turn left out of the station, opened on 22 June 1907 for the Hampstead tube, and cross the road to Marine Ices. Until the beginning of the 19th century, this was still open pasture land, part of the Blue Barn Field. From 1814 the landowner, Lord Southampton, let off the land abutting the highway on building leases. Thomas Wheeler began building 3 houses in Eschol Place at this southern end of Haverstock Hill, and in the next decade he built a row of eight 2-storey cottages here, which he naturally called Wheeler Row. Few traces now survive of Wheeler's houses, which included Bank, Sussex and Gloucester Cottages and which stood on the site of present Nos.2-18 **HAVERSTOCK HILL**. The corner house, today's No.2, was built later, shortly before Crogsland Road (p 55) had been formed. Since its construction in 1865, it has always been a beerhouse,

originally the Enterprise Tavern, and from 1953 the **Enterprise**. Notice the pub sign, whose theme – 'selling ice-cream to Inuits' – is at once a politically-incorrect gloss on the pub's name and a gentle tribute to its more famous neighbours next door. **Nos.6-8**, now home to Marine Ices, have a similar long history of refreshment provision. At No.6, in 1914, Mrs Alma Rogers took over the coffee rooms which traded under her name until 1955, while at No.8, Annabel Cartagena's fruiterers 1914-38 was the forerunner of Gaetano Mansi's fruiterers and confectioners, which became an official Ice Cream bar in 1955. Their surplus fruit was made into the water ices which established their reputation. The premises were rebuilt in 1947 to resemble the bridge of a ship. At Nos.10-16 is the **Chalk Farm Citadel** of the Salvation Army. The handsome new and welcoming building of 2004-5, designed by architects Tooley and Foster, took the place of the machicolated red fortress of 1923. Prior to that, the Army used the Hall of the Peniel Tabernacle (p 19).

Nos.20-22, two much-altered 3-storey houses incorporate elements of the original Powis Cottages of 1830. Notice the entrance veranda and the attractive ironwork. The builders C H Peppiatt & Son started their business here in 1913. Then, until 1914, back from the road, stood the appropriately named The Retreat, an equally early detached house. In 1841 it was the home of Thomas Garland, a dancing master.

Before we consider the development and complicated history of Haverstock School, whose new buildings (2004-5) by architects Fielden Clegg, Bradley now fill the road frontage, it is worth recalling their predecessors on this site. Progressive enlargement of the school site has almost obliterated the sequence of houses rejoicing in the generic title Powis Place but also individually named. Building leases were taken out in 1824 and 1825 by Thomas Brown, Joseph Griffiths and Thomas Wheeler, and Powis Place was built a couple of years later. Marsden House and Linden House, at Nos.26-28, were the first to be removed in 1902. Eton House at No.30 and Nos.32-38 were demolished in 1910. Nos.40-48 remained until 1953. Photographs taken by surveyors for the Hampstead Tube in 1903 show most of the pretentiously named houses in Powis Place as very modest affairs. Eton House was a chaste 2-storey stuccoed cottage with arched windows and dainty ironwork. Nos.32-44 were 2½-storey stuccoed cottages with slate roofs and lower linking wings and delicate ironwork. **No.50**, which remains, is more substantial, with debased ornament.

At No.36, Manor Lodge, William MacHogan was living in 1830. On 6 June 1832, with 28 others, he was elected to the St Pancras Vestry under the new Act. No.36 was from 1857 home to the Grossmith family. George Grossmith Sr (1820-80), a journalist and entertainer, described himself in the next census as a literary lecturer. Still living at home in his twenties was George Jr (1847-1912), likewise a journalist and a 'solo entertainer', whose one-man shows featured anecdotes, ad-lib chats and comic songs (see p 74). He later created many of W S Gilbert's characters for the Savoy Operas, but is best remembered for *A Diary of a Nobody*, co-authored with his brother Weedon and serialised in *Punch* in 1888-89. Satirising the social insecurity of middle-class life in the new North London suburbs, the novel (set in Holloway) might as easily have been set in Haverstock Hill. Indeed Weedon's drawing of 'The Laurels' bears more than a passing resemblance to Powis Place. In 1873 George Jr married and moved to nearby Maitland Park Villas (p 74).

At No.44 in 1871 lived Henry Court from Switzerland, a dealer in ivory. Next door, the more spacious 3-storey No.48 (Massingham House), housed a preparatory school run in 1844 by Sarah Hall, and attended by the younger George Grossmith. Twenty years later, William Debenham, photographer, lived there. No.50 had a split personality for many years, builders' merchants sharing the house with Miss Brodie's kindergarten in 1885.

Until 1871 the site of Nos.54-56 was part of the 5-acre Bedford Nursery, run by Thomas Brown in the 1820s. A large greenhouse had been built on the roadside by the time the nursery moved further up Haverstock Hill. The houses that were then built spawned lock-up shops: in 1902 Thomas Gleary, electrical engineer, was at No.56a, and Welford and Sons were running a dairy at No.58a, which supplied "absolutely pure milk". It is a relief to find that **Nos.60-62,** Augusta Villa and Marsden Villa, were substantial and dignified houses, built by Thomas Brown in 1828. No.60 carries a wall plaque to Dr Noel Farman, a family doctor who had his surgery here for 43 years until his death in 1970. A few decades earlier Mountain Patterson, surgeon-dentist, lived and practised at No.61. The last building at the corner was occupied for nearly a century until 1975 by auctioneers Dolman and Pearce, who enlarged the original 2-storey building after WWI.

Haverstock School has long dominated this portion of Haverstock Hill. Opened on 9 October 1874, it was a pioneer establishment of the School Board for London. It provided 1166 of the 8403 school places created by the Board in St Pancras in that amazing year. Initially, the school comprised a single-storey Infants school and a combined building for older boys and girls which was to attract great international attention. Designed by E R Robson before the familiar three-decker plan had been adopted, it consisted of a series of interconnected classrooms enclosing an open playground. As construction proceeded this open space was given a glass roof, creating a central hall from which the head teacher could see at a glance what was going on in every classroom, essential in those early days when there were few qualified teachers. It also provided a space for whole school assemblies. This design was so successful that halls became an indispensable element of later Board Schools. The first headmaster was the very experienced Henry Coombes, who lived in Eton House (No.30) while the school was being built in the enclosed garden ground behind. There was a "picturesque private pedestrian approach from Haverstock Hill", as well as access from Truro and Craddock Streets (pp 67 & 66).

In the first few years, the visitors included the Peruvian Minister of Education, the Emperor of Brazil and the Japanese Ambassador. In 1891 a further building was added, at Craddock Street ("up-country"), and a Manual Training Centre was opened five years later. School fees had been abolished in 1891 in London, to the relief of many parents. Coombes resigned in 1898, but continued a lively interest in

the school into his very old age. In 1904, on the site of Nos.26-28 Haverstock Hill, the School Board built a single-storey School for Physically Defective Children. Many of these suffered from the Victorian childhood disease of rickets and arrived in horse-drawn ambulances [20].

Because of vehement opposition from the Church and other reactionary forces, the School Board for London was legally unable to develop secondary education in the capital. In 1905, therefore, the School

Board handed over its responsibilities to the London County Council. The LCC introduced Central Schools, and in 1911 separate Boys and Girls Central Schools were built on the site of Nos.30-38 Haverstock Hill. The linked 3-storey blocks, designed by T J Bailey, opened on the morning of 16 January in thick fog. The electricity had not been connected, no-one could see, and all were sent home. Some years before, a similar emergency is recorded by headmaster John Sadd:

20 Haverstock Hill c.1904: a horse-drawn ambulance waits outside the School for Physically Defective Children

"I wired the Board this morning at 8.40 a.m. No coal, 27 open fires and 4 stoves".

By 1914 there were seven separate schools sharing this site. During WWI 400 ex-pupils joined up, and 1 staff member and 42 ex-pupils were killed. The Central Schools, meanwhile, were encouraged to experiment with the curriculum. The Girls School, as well as making gas masks and knitting socks was developing French language teaching throughout the school, and discouraging competitiveness in games! This, the Inspectors admitted, was an excellent school, but perhaps "not quite what the Authority had in mind". The original 1874 buildings were replaced between 1915 and 1920. A school keeper's house was added in 1923.

At the outbreak of WWII Haverstock School was evacuated to Luton, but the London buildings were used for a Wartime Emergency School (1941-1945). In 1941 the Special School, which was being used as education offices, was demolished by a landmine and not reopened. A school dining hall was built on the site in 1943, in temporary buildings that lasted over 60 years. In 1945, the Central Schools and Elementary and Infants Schools reopened. The Infants School closed in 1948.

In September 1949, Haverstock reopened as an experimental 8-form Comprehensive School, "although the accommodation fell strikingly short of what was needed, even of the most modest kind, for 1400 pupils". The much-needed new buildings were slow to appear. The first of 2 gymnasia (3 were planned) was completed in 1957 on the site of Nos.40-48 Haverstock Hill, and science, workshops and administration in Crogsland Road followed in 1959. The school successfully defied all attempts to close it in the 1970s and 1980s, but in spite of its success, the expenditure required for the major improvements was not forthcoming. By 2000 it was clear that only a completely new building would equip the school for another century of endeavour, and at the time of writing that is being constructed.

Now cross over Prince of Wales Road (p 66) to the Adventist church. Before entering Maitland Park, we continue up the east side of Haverstock Hill as far as **No.84a**, close to the next bus stop. Here was the original boundary between St Pancras and Hampstead. This strip was transferred from St Pancras to Hampstead in 1900 as one result of the 1899 Local Government Act. In 1804 it was still part of a meadow called Moll King's Field. Born in St Giles, Mary, Moll or 'Mother' King (1696−1747), who as a child sold fruit from a barrow in Covent Garden, went on to become a wealthy businesswoman, and the proprietor of that district's most successful (and disorderly) coffee house. Here on Haverstock Hill, just short of the Hampstead border and the Load of Hay pub (now The Hill), she erected, with her husband Tom, three substantial houses. For her favourite protégée, Nancy Dawson, she built a small villa, set back from the road. Nancy was a famous hornpipe dancer at Covent Garden Theatre, who gave memorable performances in John Gay's *Beggar's Opera*. She died at her house in 1767, and is buried in St George's Gardens (Bloomsbury). Two of the houses built by Moll King are almost certainly **Nos.82-84**, 4-storey and taller than their neighbours. No.84 (Cheriton House) was the family and business home of Frank Galliard, whose wine-importing activities were based here for over 45 years. Walk back down the hill, passing No.82 (Forres House), the home from 1870 to 1906 of Thomas Hutchings, boot maker. The third house, No.80, was demolished in 1880 for Dawson Terrace, an imposing late-Victorian row built in recently cleaned stock brick; its name and its date 1882 (in Roman numerals) is displayed above **No.76**. The 1870 map shows the former No.80 to have had a street frontage, a large garden and a villa at the back. That villa still exists, and will be seen as we walk through Maitland Park. It seems to be a modest 2-storey white stuccoed building with a slate mansard roof, quite different from Dawson Terrace. It could well be Nancy Dawson's house. William Hogarth clearly shows these buildings on Haverstock Hill on the right of his painting

The March to Finchley in the Foundling Museum. In 1861, No.80 was occupied by Haverstock School (not to be confused with the later Board School) run by Hannah Burr, with 13 scholars and 4 staff.

Continue down the hill to reach **No.70**, the imposing former Vicarage of Holy Trinity (Clarence Way), built in 1867 on the site of Field Cottage. Designed by architects Beck and Lee, it was built by B Webb & Sons for £2879. Note the sculpted portcullis and Tudor rose referring to the Duke of Westminster who helped pay for it, as did collections from concerts at the Queen's Hall. The vicarage was converted into flats in 1994. **Nos.68&68a** are surprising. Two suburban houses of 1933, they displaced Holywell House and Holywell Cottage. The Music Hall artiste Gertie Gitana, who popularised the song *Nellie Dean,* lived at No.68a for a while and named the house Neldean. Holywell House appears on the 1804 map. Benjamin Cant, a tobacconist, was living there in 1885, after which the place seems to have fallen into neglect. It was a beautiful, small stuccoed villa, with a pediment and an elaborate first-floor balcony, and stood well back from the road.

The last building before the turning is the **Seventh Day Adventist Church** which moved here from Regent Street in 1972. The building was formerly the Oxendon Presbyterian Church, built on the site of Pulvin Cottage, occupied in 1864 by George Vinall, Gentleman. The church had its origins in a chapel built in Oxendon Street (Westminster) for the great 17th-century divine, Richard Baxter. Baxter was forcibly denied the use of his chapel by Charles II, but a congregation continued there until, in the 19th century, it left the depopulated area for Haverstock Hill; a new church, designed by Thomas Arnold, was built here in 1877. The congregation moved on again in 1970, merging with that of Trinity Church, Camden Town.

As you turn left round the end of the church, notice the two boundary markers from 1899/1900. Keep to the left and walk up **MAITLAND PARK ROAD** past two short terraces of flats on your left through which it is possible to see the white house of Nancy Dawson in the trees. The best view is at **Nos.199-205**. The road now forks. Maitland Park Road continues to the right, and we shall explore that section on the return leg of our walk. Keep to the roadway to the left, which is **MAITLAND PARK VILLAS**. Notice on the right the sculpture *Family Group* (of c.1960). It stands on the site of Maitland Park House (No.1A), one of the largest houses on the estate. This was once home to Levi Cottrell, the widowed former landlord (in 1843-60) of the well-known Britannia public house in Camden Town.

Continue to the entrance gateway to **Alexandra House**, which is now a day centre. Until 1939 this was the main entrance to the Orphan Working School. This area was briefly known as Haverstock Park, when in 1841 the school purchased 12½ acres of pasture land from Lord Southampton for £5,580. The Orphan Working School was founded in 1758 in Hoxton to provide schooling and employment opportunities for orphan children. The first pupils, 130 boys and 100 girls, moved into the new school building here, designed by Alfred Ainger [21], in September 1847.

The school occupied 6 acres of the site; the remainder was let out on building leases for villas. In 1853, the name Maitland Park was officially adopted as a tribute to the Maitland family who had been the main support of the charity from 1765 to 1834. Charles Dickens was a Life Governor, whose 5-guinea subscription entitled him to nominate prospective inmates. The Orphan Working School was renamed the Alexandra Orphanage in 1924 in honour of Edward VII's consort, and the Royal Alexandra School in 1944. But by then it was no longer at Maitland Park. On 1 September 1939, the school was evacuated out of London, and after WWII re-established in Surrey. Foreseeing such a move, the London County Council bought the whole Maitland Park site in February 1939, and it is mainly their buildings that we see today. Looking through the entrance to the left, we can see the former Infirmary (1906) by architects Young and Hall, with additions, which is now the Council-run Alexandra Day Centre.

The opposite (east) side of the road once contained the best houses on the estate. At the south end six pairs of villas were strategically sited to set off the school buildings opposite. At No.4, the writer and publisher James Camden Hotten (b.1832) died in 1873. His original middle name was William, and it is unknown why and when he adopted the locally interesting substitute. Always a risk-taker, he had nobly published Swinburne's *Poems and Ballads* (1866) when the original publisher got cold feet, while his somewhat less noble later publications included works on aphrodisiacs, phallic worship and flagellation. After Hotten's untimely

21   The Orphan Working School, 'moving from the City Road' (architect's drawing c.1847)

death (aged 40), his widow sold the business to his clerk, Andrew Chatto, who went into partnership with one William Windus. Resident at No.6 for over 40 years was Rev. John Nunn (1861-1909), minister of the neighbouring Haverstock Hill Congregational Church (p 82). A very large villa at No.7 initially housed Charles Tuckett, a St Giles-born master bookbinder sufficiently well-heeled to employ both a nurse and an under-nurse to care for his children. The 1871 census shows him here with his wife, 2 sons, 5 daughters and 3 servants and records that he employed 55 men, 15 women and 3 boys. From c.1885 the house belonged to the watercolour painter Robert Thorne Waite (1842-1935). He described his studio here as "big enough for a military painter", although landscapes and seascapes were his own forte. After WWI, the artist Percyval Tudor-Hart moved in. At No.13, the first of the terraced houses, Hannah Burr was living in 1871, having moved her school (p 72) from Haverstock Hill. Another exile from Haverstock Hill was George Grossmith Jr [22], who upon his marriage to Emmeline Noyce in 1873 moved into No.15. Born here in 1874 was the third George Grossmith, the future playwright and actor-manager, who wrote libretti for musicals and co-founded the Winter Garden theatre in Drury Lane. No.16 was home for a while to the architect Samuel Knight. From c.1867 No.17 was home

22 George Grossmith (1847-1912), co-author of *Diary of a Nobody* (1888-9), pictured at the age of 25 (from *Strand Magazine* Aug 1891)

to Sister Rose's Foundation, a group of nuns from a convent at Stroud (Glos.), which for a few years provided teachers for St Dominic's (p 75). They later moved to No.25, where four nuns were still in residence in 1871. Another religious order, of nursing sisters – the Convent of Bon Secours – flourished from 1874 at No.21. The Established Church occupied No.24 as the Vicarage of St Andrew's Church, Haverstock Hill during the incumbency (1884-1906) of Rev. George Blaxland.

This (west) side of the road is today lined by six blocks of flats built in 1948-52 by the LCC Housing Department in their typical pre-War style. The blocks run parallel to the road in groups of three. The first three are called **Willow**, **Sycamore**, and **Maple** Houses, while the next group's arboreal names are **Oak**, **Chestnut**, and **Beech**. The next block, **Aspen House**, was an afterthought. The original LCC plan for the Estate was for a community centre here, but this was abandoned in favour of more flats. Aspen House was built in 1968 to the design of the architects Jan Farber and Bartholomew. It stands on the site of the Orphan Working School's Chapel, built in 1881 to a design by Charles Bell "in a free treatment of Italian style". It had accommodation for 500 visitors and 300 children, with separate entrances, and a good-sized organ chamber. Its final function was as a store for a film company.

Turn left at Aspen House and walk up to the **Maitland Park Gymnasium**, constructed along the parish boundary in a corner of the old school playground. It was a memorial to Lord Marshall, a long-time treasurer of the Orphan Working School institution. It was opened by his daughter, Mrs J Arthur Rank, in 1937 and became the last gift from the school to the locality.

After WWII it was used by Fleet Road and Haverstock Schools, neither of which had a gymnasium. It is now part of Camden's community provision.

Returning to the road, we continue north past two earlier LCC blocks, **Alder House** and **Hornbeam House**, to the grounds of another local charity, the St Pancras Almshouses at the south end of **SOUTHAMPTON ROAD**. The almshouses opened in 1852 in what became Wilkin Street (p 51) and were transferred to new buildings on this site, acquired from a Mr Thompson for £1300, in 1860. The present almshouses are called **Fraser Regnart Court**, after their founder, churchwarden Dr Donald Fraser, together with their major benefactor Horatio Regnart who was also a president of the furniture makers Maple's. The buildings were designed by Henry Baker FRIBA, whose memorial tablet in St Pancras Parish Church records that he was District Surveyor of St Pancras for 53 years. This delightful quadrangle with its lawns, Tudor decoration and Listed lamp standards, seems an even more telling memorial to him.

Across Southampton Road the tiled **Lord Southampton** pub reminds us that all this land was originally his. The pub is said to have been a favourite drinking-place of Marx and Engels (p 87). The adjacent terrace at **Nos.4-18**, 2½-storey

and stuccoed, with taller end houses, was built as Fitzroy Terrace in 1856; it retains some good ironwork. **Nos.20-38**, a 3-storey stock-brick row leading up to the Malden Road junction, dates from 1859-61 and briefly enjoyed the name Bickerton Terrace. Bickerton Hill (Cheshire) lies near to the parish of Malpas of which the Rev. Charles Thurlow (see Thurlow Terrace, p 79) was rector.

On the left-hand side after Fraser Regnart Court, the yellow brick bulk of **Wordsworth Place** rises on the site of the Blackfriars Hall, one of the pioneer buildings of **St Dominic's Priory**, and which housed its school until 1932. The gables of Wordsworth Place, completed in 1997, at least acknowledge the gabled roofscape of the Priory itself. In 1861 Cardinal Wiseman invited the Dominicans to establish a major Roman Catholic Centre here. They bought the 3-acre site in the following year, and the first stone was laid in 1863. The first buildings for the Community, including the clock tower, were completed in 1867, and the library on the first floor at first served as the church.

The Priory Church of Our Lady of the Rosary and St Dominic was designed by the architect Gilbert Blount, who died in 1876 and was succeeded by Charles Alban Buckler. There were continual conflicts over the cost of the church. 'As much as possible for as little as possible' was the order of the day and Buckler's church, 299

ft long and over 80 ft high, led to questions in the House of Commons as well as comments that "the Papists had erected a dangerous building".

The side chapels serve to buttress the main external walls. Because of the constraints of the site, the High Altar is, unusually, at the West end. The church still retains many of its contemporary furnishings. Chief among them is the superb 4-manual 'Father' Willis organ, made in the Rotunda Works, Kentish Town and installed in 1883 and because it is still essentially in its original condition, historically one of the more important instruments in the country. Since 2000, regular recitals have been a feature here. The church was finally opened in 1883, when the Bishop of Clifton celebrated Pontifical High Mass and Gounod's *New Mass* was sung. The ceremony attracted great interest.

Notice, too, the War Memorial with lettering by Joseph Cribb, a pupil of Eric Gill. Beyond the church, turn left into **Alan Cheales Way**, a footpath which leads to Tasker Road (formerly Church Road) in Hampstead. Alan Cheales OP was a much-loved prior and parish priest (who reverted to his own name from that of Fr John Dominic after Vatican 2). He died in 1996 after 34 years' service (usually by bicycle) to the locality. At his funeral service, he was described as "a great oak".

From the path, the lower ashlar stone

wall of Gilbert Blount's church can be seen. This path became a through route to Southampton Road only in 1932 when the Church School moved into its new building on the site of the Brothers' garden. Return to Southampton Road and turn left. High on the façade of **St Dominic's Primary School and Nursery** are three statues – the Virgin and child in the centre, flanked by two saints.

Beyond the school we come to **Nos.1-15** Southampton Road. This is a row of 3-storey shops built in 1852, somewhat battered, but with several original shop fronts. Notice "C J Hairdressers, established 1906", and then in the pavement outside No.15, the Inspection Cover of the "LCC Tramways". This was probably installed to control the points where the tracks were singled at a tramway 'pinch'. It reminds us of the importance of tramways in the development of Gospel Oak. A single-track horse tramway reached this point in 1880 and provided a regular service of blue cars to King's Cross and of yellow cars to Euston, both travelling via Kentish Town. This tramway was extended to South End Green, Hampstead in 1886, after which Holborn was added to the destinations served. In 1894, the LCC won control of the system, and in 1909 the operation was electrified. The Hampstead routes were converted to trolleybus operation in 1938, but the tram rails were left in place to serve the depot in

Fleet Road, which was used as a tram store until 1947. The rails were finally taken up in 1953, and the last trolleybus ran to the Hampstead terminus in 1961.

Still in Southampton Road, **No.17** with an extra floor turns the corner into **KINGSFORD STREET**. This street dates from 1871, when the first five houses on the north side, **Nos.1-5**, were completed. This is on land which was sold as Lot 1 in the 1840 sale of the Southampton lands. Advertised as suitable for 15 villas at a price of £1,000, it was bought by John Jay. The land on the south side of the street was used for various commercial purposes, notably Samuel Smith's carpet-beating establishment, which survived until 1921. In its last decade it was "steam-powered". Attempts to restrict this noisy and dirty activity failed because it operated only between 6 am and 8 pm! Other industrial concerns in the 1950s were Peters Brothers' egg-packing depot and the coachworks of Sidney Marriott, motor bodywork engineers. In 2002 the street was transformed. **Nos. 6-12** on the north side have pleasant oriel windows, and those on the south side are grouped with commercial premises built on the site of a former metal-working yard. In 1931 the sculptor Frazer Blundell is recorded as working here.

Returning to **SOUTHAMPTON ROAD**, we pass **Nos.19-23** before reaching the brick parapet of a railway bridge. On the north side of the bridge, a

controlled entrance with trees leads into Dunboyne flats. This is the site of the Gospel Oak. Not much is known of this tree, or of its significance, save that it gave its name to the area, Gospel Oak Fields. The St Pancras Vestry Minutes record in the 1827 Perambulation of the Boundaries "a boundary stone close to the paling enclosing the Gospel Oak Tree", although minutes of the perambulation 6 years previously make it clear that the tree itself had disappeared by 1821. A short sermon was preached to the assembled party during this beating of the bounds; John Richardson has suggested that the tree was the site for this sermon, hence the name Gospel Oak. In 1854, Churchwarden Billet moved in Vestry "that a Stone be erected on the spot in Gospel Oak Field, Kentish Town where the Old Oak stood". He called for a design to be prepared for Vestry approval. There is no record that this was done.

The Old Oak fell, or was destroyed, sometime before 1821 but it had served as a boundary mark for many years – it is shown on the 1801 parish map – and it may well have been a gathering place for outdoor preaching. Both George Whitefield and John Wesley spoke to large gatherings in 'Marylebone Fields', but specific references to 'Gospel Oak' are scanty except in mentions of the annual Easter fair held "in the fields" until at least 1857. This was finally suppressed under the Act authorising the Midland Railway's line into London. Perhaps Mr Billet's stone, if it was erected, also fell victim to the Midland Railway's drive through Gospel Oak in the 1860s, but there is no excuse for the removal of the St Pancras/St John Hampstead boundary stone, which could be seen near the site of the Old Oak until a few years ago.

The railway bridge spans the Midland main line just before the tracks plunge into the tunnels underneath Hampstead. The first tunnel, 'Belsize No.1', was begun in a snowstorm in January 1865 and completed in December 1867. The contract price was £238,741 18s 6d. The tunnel is 1 mile 26 yards long, it runs 120 ft below ground and has a ruling gradient of 1 in 182. An average of 1,000 men and 160 horses were employed on the works; six shafts were sunk and 22 million bricks were used. Workers were injured and lives lost. Joseph Butt, 21, fell down a shaft on 1 September 1866 and William Cook, a miner, was killed in the tunnel on 24 November 1866. Traffic over the Midland Railway's London Extension began on 1 October 1868, and Haverstock Hill Station (p 87) came to life at the same time. The disruption from the building of the first tunnel was enormous, but traffic, especially carrying coal, grew at such a rate that the provision of a second, parallel, tunnel, for which authority had been obtained, was accelerated, and construction began in 1880. This time there were more protests, as the Midland

laid a series of light railways across Southampton Road and through the streets of Gospel Oak to the massive spoil heap where the excavated clay would be turned into bricks. But the Vestry was dilatory and failed to confront the railway with their breaches of contract. This second tunnel was finished in 1884. It had cost £257,942 17s 6d. The engineers for both bores were Barlow and Baker.

A minor casualty of Belsize No.2 was the last street in our northward journey, Dunboyne Street, named after a village near Dublin with a remote Fitzroy family connection (Georgiana Fitzroy, daughter of the 2nd Lord Southampton, married a descendant of the 16th-century 9th Lord of Dunboyne). It first appears in 1871 (between tunnels), with 6 houses on the north side, and 2 houses and a scrap-yard on the south. By 1891 only the north side is left. Together with another small area of backland called Southampton Mews, and later home to piano-action repairers F W Carter & Sons, the whole block was redeveloped after WWII. **DUNBOYNE ROAD**, the present elegant white-walled scheme designed by Neave Brown in 1966, but not built until 1969, with precise elevations and ingenious planning for 73 flats with garages and a communal roof garden, has influenced later schemes in Camden and elsewhere. Only the unfinished ramps to the never-executed bridge over Southampton

Road leave a question mark.

Cross over to the east side of **SOUTHAMPTON ROAD**, where the Mansfield Hotel (p 104) formerly stood, and turn right to return towards the Priory, noticing in the distance the great length of the church. Today the east side of the road is part of the Gospel Oak Estate (Route 5). The houses once leading down to the railway line were undistinguished 3-storey terraced houses, built on land owned by Messrs Brown and Griffiths in 1865. Between No.82 and No.86 a Congregational chapel was built. Its founder R H Smith, who had been apprenticed to a printer, moved to Gospel Oak from Surbiton, where he had built a small church in 1865. The congregation first met in the two rooms and conservatory of his house at No.80. The chapel was funded by the London Chapels Building Society and gifts from Samuel Morley and others. It was a Romanesque style building, consisting of a single space with two aisles and galleries on cast-iron columns, a double porch and a large rose window. The architect was W Allen Dixon. A schoolroom was added in 1869. The church was active in its ministry to the navvies engaged on the second Belsize tunnel and to the tramway community. R H Smith left in 1881 and died in 1885, when the St Pancras Vestry Hall was host to a benefit concert for his family. The church closed in 1937 and the building became an LCC Restaurant. It was demolished, with the rest of Gospel Oak Area 9, in 1969.

At the railway bridge notice the mural painting on the parapets and the more recent Guantanamo-style security fencing. Nine newly completed houses were demolished here in 1864-65 by the Midland Railway which wisely purchased sufficient land for a four-track formation, including the Belsize No.2 tunnel. Beyond was a terrace of 9 houses, Nos.64-80, and a public house, the Gospel Oak. The latter was built in 1856 on the corner of Rochford Street, then called Circus Road, which led to Lismore Circus (p 85). It was licensed as a theatre from 1856 to 1869. The Gospel Oak pub, if architecturally nondescript, could at least claim to be the closest refreshment site to the historic tree. It lasted until 1970 and **Wendling** (p 95) now covers the site. Today, replacement oak trees are thriving near the bridge. During the building of the second tunnel, the light railway from the tunnel workings to the brickfield site ran along Rochford Street. However inconvenient it must have been, it probably provided good business for the pub. Cross over the rump of former Rochford Street, the unmarked **NEW ROCHFORD STREET**, which now simply leads alongside Wendling. Beyond Rochford Street there were 4 houses before Piercefield Street (p 94) and a further block of six called Piercefield Terrace, taking us

to the junction with Malden Road.

Cross over the road; the tree in the central reservation is another memorial to Fr. Alan Cheales. Turn left down **MALDEN ROAD**, initially built up from its southern end (Route 3). We are concerned with the last two terraces on the west side, constructed in the 1860s. Malden Road is first recorded as an unnamed thoroughfare shown on the Southampton Estate sale map of 1840. The many individual terrace names were abolished in 1863 when it officially assumed its present name, deriving from another estate, at (New) Malden in Surrey, given by Charles II to his son Henry Fitzroy, the ancestor of Lord Southampton. Although building was completed by 1870, the development was not without its critics. The paving, or lack of it, was a sore point. In 1856 a correspondent had complained: "there are 230 houses empty for want of proper roads, Malden Road (sic) is dangerous and deplorable". A later writer described the situation in 1880: "the larger portion of Malden Road was occupied by shops and private houses gradually being converted into shops, and it would at some time become a great thoroughfare".

The first terrace we reach, **Nos.143-181**, was completed in 1861. It was then known as Kingsbridge Terrace, a plain 3-storey brick range. One wonders whether the builder James Ponsford (see p 61) had a hand in its construction. Kingsbridge is

the nearest town to Modbury, the South Devon village from which the Ponsford family hailed; Thomas Ponsford, a relation of James, was the architect of the town's workhouse. The first four houses, Nos.175-181, have remained residential. Note on **No.175** and **No.179** the pretty, floreate iron balconettes. Most of the rest are shops; when the buildings were auctioned off in March 1861 they were stated to be "built with bresimers [sic] so as to be easily convertible into shops". The corner house, **No.143**, looks as though it might have been a pub. In fact, it was the local bakery started by George Whiting in 1862 and continued until 1940. John Granger was the baker for 31 years until 1905, when it was briefly under German ownership. After WWII it was converted into flats.

Turn right into Malden Place and right again to explore the charming enclave of **QUADRANT GROVE**. The origin of the name is obscure. It has been suggested that the houses **Nos.2, 4**, and **6** form a quadrant, or one fourth of a circle, of which the 3 remaining sectors were never built, or that the intended layout has been altered. A simpler explanation is that the area on the northern side of the central street, bounded on one side by the curved end of Malden Road, approximates to a quadrant. The earliest houses are the pleasant, large-eaved, double pair of villas at **Nos.23-29**, built in 1849 at the Southampton Road end. In 1851, No.27 was the home of

Paterson Boyle, umbrella manufacturer, his wife, 2 children and 2 servants. It was nearly 20 years before the remaining houses were completed.

Return along this leafy grove to **MALDEN PLACE**. This piece of backland is now filled by a block of flats, built in 1982. The land was owned in 1859 by Dr Henry Guard Knaggs (p 37), but the first record of any resident here was in 1881 when the sole house was occupied by Thomas Bromfield, a cowkeeper. His cows probably occupied the rest of the site. In 1891, Bromfield is shown as a milk dairyman. Ten years later the family breadwinner is his son Arthur, a coachsmith. By 1931, the site has been totally enclosed as a motor garage. Its final commercial use was from 1953 as a depot for MacFisheries who stored their returned empty boxes there.

Back in **MALDEN ROAD**, we turn right and follow the next terrace (**Nos.119-141**) southward. Note the stucco embellishments to the windows, and that the two shops by the corner, **Nos.135-139**, are stuccoed all over. These houses originally formed St George's Terrace, while the whole curving northern end of Malden Road was known until 1863 as St George's Crescent.

Continue to **No.129**. Here in 1863-64 was the studio of the Swedish artist Oscar Gustav Rejlander (1817-75), painter turned pioneer photographer. Rejlander was the son of a Swedish army officer who studied in Rome. In England he was first a portrait painter and then a photographer. He resolved "to do what had never been done" and produced, as a first offering, the *Two Ways of Life*, which caused great controversy when exhibited in 1857. A 'combination print' compiled from over 30 negatives, it was too contrived for his colleagues and, in its lifelike depiction of nudity, too risqué for the public. He continued to find subjects among the discarded victims of poverty. No.129 today, as St Joseph's House, is the headquarters of the Simon Community. Founded in 1963 by Anton Wallich-Clifford, the Community works with street sleepers and the homeless. At the next corner is the former Malden Arms. This pub was built in 1867 by Frederick Holsworth for £2,517. It closed in 1996 and was converted into flats, like so many of its contemporaries.

Turn right into exceptionally wide **GRAFTON TERRACE**, renamed in 1872 after the Duke of Grafton, head of the Fitzroy family. Originally called Fitzroy Road, the street was lined by houses previously known as Clifton Terrace and Grafton Villas. At No.4 Grafton Villas in 1867 lived the painter Edward Deanes. The first five houses, with ironwork balconies, on the south side and the houses on the north side of the street were completed in 1855.

Cross to the south side, where we pass on the left the gap that was once Chaston Street. This short street of 10 houses had been originally named Millman Street, but was renamed in 1885 after Edward Chaston, Manager of the National Bank, Camden High Street, who owned several plots of land in this area. The houses were built in 1871. In 1887, the parents of Ada Neil, aged 4 months, who lived at No.9, were charged with manslaughter for allowing her to die of neglect. Her father was a horse-clipper. Booth in 1898 called the street "very rough and low". The houses were demolished in 1969 and the site became an open space. In 2002 the **Chaston Nursery and Pre-Preparatory School** was built here. Its sign obscures, but does not totally cover, the old wall-painted name of Chaston Street. The nursery's postal address is 'Chaston Place'.

The following seven houses, **Nos.25-37**, form a pleasant, unified terrace and lead us to the next turning left, **THURLOW TERRACE**. Two clerical gentlemen of this name, the Rev. Edward Thurlow and Charles Thurlow, rector of Malpas in Cheshire, negotiated with Lord Southampton for the land in 1856. The houses date from 1860. But notice the hall, resembling a Robson Board school, attached to the corner house in **GRAFTON TERRACE**. This tall, stuccoed house, **No.39**, boasts some arched windows, a columned porch and entrance steps. It is now the Hindu Centre. It was built in 1857 for Charles Gay and rejoiced in the loyal name of Osborne House, appearing on contemporary maps as a detached property of some pretension, if not distinction. From 1891 it became an outstation of the London City Mission, and the hall was built for them. After they left, some 20 years later, it became a Free Gospel Hall.

The terrace opposite, on the north side, at **Nos.30-60**, has a very unusual design. The grouped doorways have curved steps and the treatment of the arched upper windows is very strange, with an insistent pattern of windows. Such houses were being let by the floor by 1898, when Booth noted Inspector Tomkin's comment that there were many disturbances in the street and labelled it "rough". In the 1860s it was a slightly better neighbourhood. To our right, at **No.34** (then No.3), William Frederick Settle (1821-97), marine painter of Hull, lived from 1865 to 1868. **No.46** (previously No.9) was the first St Pancras home of the most noteworthy resident of this area, Herr Doktor Karl Marx **[23]**.

After the *Communist Manifesto* was published in 1848, Marx left the Continent as a political exile and, with his family, made his home in London. He moved here from Soho in 1855 with his wife Jenny and their three surviving daughters. Confusingly, all of the Marx daughters were named Jenny, after their mother. The eldest and best known, the future

23 Karl Marx (1818-1883) in 1861

socialist writer and activist (Jenny Julia) Eleanor Marx, was then only nine months old. Always strapped for cash and heavily dependent on Friedrich Engels, who lived not far away in Regent's Park Road. Marx was able to move here thanks to a legacy. For this new, unfurnished house, he paid £36 per annum. In 1855, however, "this end of Hampstead is somewhat unfinished. Our house not easy to get to …building was going on all around…and in rainy weather the sticky red soil caked one's boots…and then it was dark in those wild districts". In the 1861 census he is shown as Karl Mara [sic], Doctor of Philosophy,

head of a household which at that time included his wife, three daughters and two sons. Until 1862 Marx eked out his income by journalistic work as the European correspondent for the *New York Daily Tribune*, while also spending long hours at the British Library Reading Room preparing two major works of economic theory: *Grundrisse der Kritik der politischen Ökonomie* (1857-58) and *Zur Kritik der politischen Ökonomie* (1859). In 1863 Marx was elected a Constable of the Vestry of St Pancras, a sinecure which he did not take up, quoting the advice of an Irish neighbour: "I should tell them that I was a foreigner, and that they should kiss me on the arse". An inheritance in 1864 enabled the family to move 'up market', and we shall meet again very shortly.

Former No.53, on the left, was home shortly after WWI to the artist Carl Almquist, but by 1937 housed Senger Manufacturing, makers of megaphones. The site is now covered by the **Maitland Park Community Garden**, "a dog-free zone". The garden is at the end of the street. We however turn left, beyond **No.43**, to re-enter the LCC's Maitland Park Estate. This semi-pedestrianised section of **MAITLAND PARK ROAD** is modern, having been cut through the site of a onetime stable yard. Walk past the flats on the right at **Nos.109-134**.

Beyond these, and to your right, Maitland Park Road once continued northwest to meet Maitland Park Villas at its junction with Grafton Terrace. In that stretch, at No.53, lived the medallist Allan Wyon, Her Majesty's Chief Engraver of Seals. Born there in 1881 was his eldest daughter Olive (d.1966), the theologian, pioneer ecumenist, and eventual radio broadcaster. Although later well travelled, she was kept at home between the ages of 20 and 25, housekeeping, sick visiting and serving as missionary secretary at the Haverstock Hill Congregational Church (p 82). Her *Dawn Wind* (1931) was a feminist study of the role of women in African and Asian cultures. With no university education, but with a natural gift for languages, Olive became regarded as one of the world's ablest translators. The Swiss theologian Emil Brunner declared that her translations of his works were sometimes more intelligible than his original German. Today, the vanished stretch of road has been replaced by the grass that surrounds the 6-storey block known as **Whitebeam House**.

To our left, the east side of Maitland Park Road is lined by further flats built in 1959-64 by the LCC. Notice how the frontage here curves back from the line of the road. This is the site of Maitland Park Crescent, a west-facing arc of 14 terrace houses, completed in 1862 and labelled on one early map as 'The Quadrant'. The houses were renumbered in 1868 as part of Maitland Park Road, becoming Nos.32-45. No.41 Maitland Park Road was the Marx family's third and last local home, to which they moved in 1875 from the superior No.1, at the far end of the road (see later). Karl's wife Jenny died of liver cancer at No.41 in December 1881, leaving her husband bereft. On 14 March 1883 Karl also passed away here, sitting in his favourite easy chair. He was buried in Highgate Cemetery, in the plot where the body of his wife had been laid 18 months earlier. Only 11 mourners accompanied the coffin. French, Russian and American newspapers published suitable eulogies, but in England the death of this principal theorist of revolutionary socialism was hardly noticed.

A Camden Council brown plaque, erected in 1983 on the present maisonettes at **Nos.101-107**, recalls the family's residence. An earlier LCC plaque, affixed to the original house in 1935, was removed after having twice been vandalised. Also in the former Crescent, the playwright, poet and journalist Robert Brough had died in 1870 at No.37. In his *Songs of the Governing Classes* (1855), he had ignored the patriotic fervour aroused by the Crimean War to launch a fierce attack on the hypocrisy and inadequacy of the ruling class. Living at No.4 Maitland Park Crescent in 1864 was Edmund Thomas Parris (1793-1873), the architect and painter who in 1831 had completed Thomas Horner's unfinished panorama of London as sketched from the dome of St Paul's. He later invented Parris's Medium, a substance which when mixed with oil produced a dull fresco-like surface. Louisa Browning (b.1807), who died aged 90 at No.1, was a half-aunt of the poet Robert Browning, and a retired headmistress, whose boarding-school at Blackheath had among its pupils both Elizabeth Garrett (Anderson) and her sister Millicent, known respectively for their later promotion of women's medicine and of female higher education. Louisa was a lady of ample build and unorthodox ways: French was the language of all "transactions" at her school, and the teaching of needlework was taboo.

Houses on the west side, once facing the Crescent at Nos.57-67, were at first known as 'Maitland Park Villas (Lower Road)', and then as 'The Villas, Maitland Park Road'. Laura Villa here was home in 1867 to Rev. Septimus Buss, vicar of Holy Trinity and lifelong helper of his sister Frances Mary at the North London Collegiate School for Girls which she founded. To the south of The Villas, the west side was undeveloped, and lined by the generous back gardens of houses in Maitland Park Villas (p 73).

We are now walking south alongside an extended block of flats built by the LCC in

1959-1964. The pitched roofs and other unnecessary 'embellishments' added in 1991 do not entirely invalidate the cleaner detailing that also characterises the 6-storey 'point blocks' on the west side of the road: Whitebeam House (which we noticed before); **Rowan House** and **Hazel House**.

On our outward journey we concentrated on the history of the Orphan Working School itself. Now it is appropriate to consider the development of the residential estate that provided its income. Unfortunately, the builders who took the land for housing were under-capitalised, and frequently failed. This had serious financial consequences as well as for the physical realisation of the design. By 1855, after two years, only seven houses had been completed. By 1861, 39 were occupied. It was 1870 before the whole estate of 102 houses had been finished. It was, and is, a beautiful site, and some of the houses were villas of a goodly size, most of them built around the main entrance to the school. Here in Maitland Park Road, the houses were built as a continuous terrace, were cheaper, and consequently attracted a different clientele: ladies "living on their own means", craftsmen, and a significant number of boarding houses; by 1898 Booth noted many "apartment notices" in the windows. Multiple occupation became the norm.

On the east side, a long Maitland Park Terrace became Nos.3-31. Living in the 1860s at No.17 was William Wood Deane (1825-73), an architect turned painter, of mainly architectural subjects, whose best-known picture is his *Bull Ring at Seville*. At No.4, and at the same time, was an academy run by Thomas Upton and named Carlton House School.

We pass Maitland Park Villas (p 72) and next on the left, opposite today's 2-storey **Nos.206-209**, stood **[24]** the Haverstock Hill Congregational Chapel (John Nunn's charge). This was designed by the architects Barry and Brown of Liverpool, and completed in 1849 at a cost of £2,681. It was closed in 1946. A substantial Sunday school was built on the adjacent site. The church was erected on land bought from the Orphan Working School, and as the School was of the Congregational persuasion, the church

24 Haverstock Hill Congregational Chapel, 1850

obtained the land for a modest premium and at a peppercorn rent. In addition, before the School Chapel was built, its pupils attended Sunday worship here. They complained of the stifling heat that built up during the sermon. After closure, the church was used as an LCC Restaurant and Supplies Depot before being demolished in 1952. Abutting the Sunday School, and where now stand the 6-storey red-brick mansion flats dating from 1900 and called **The Grange**, were two houses known as Modena Villas, and also Nos.1-2 Maitland Park Road. Karl Marx and his family moved to No.1 in 1864 from Fitzroy Road (now Grafton Terrace, p 80). A year later, the ratepayer was recorded as "Charles Marx". Karl toiled at this time in the British Museum, often for 12 hours a day, on *Das Kapital* (1867), the first volume of which was published while he was living here. His notoriously untidy first-floor study, which looked along Haverstock Hill, was to become the focal point of the First International, founded in September 1864, whose proceedings were soon dominated by Marx. From 1870 the house was a conveniently short walk from the Primrose Hill home of Friedrich Engels, whom Karl met almost daily. He would never have survived his London years without Engels' intellectual support and material assistance, the latter sometimes in the form of cases of wine! The Marx family's lifestyle was unorthodox

by the standards of Haverstock Hill. The three daughters once gave a party here for 50 of their friends, which lasted until 4 am. One daughter described the house as a "veritable palace and far too expensive". The family were indeed living beyond their means, and in 1875, although the two elder daughters were by then married, and with Marx's health deteriorating and his application for British citizenship refused, they were forced to move 'down market' again, to No.41 (see above).

On the corner of Prince of Wales Road, we pass the flats of **Silverbirch Walk**, designed by Renton Howard Wood Associates, and built for the GLC in 1972. The massing of its yellow brickwork sits very happily on the corner site.

Before we leave Maitland Park altogether, notice in front of the Adventist church (p 72), the original estate name stone from 1853, which still commemorates its later owners, the London County Council. When the Council was abolished in 1964 after a life of 75 years, it was described as "one of the greatest local authorities in the world". Maitland Park was one of the few significant LCC estates in St Pancras, and it is a pleasant conjunction of history that here we can still celebrate a link between Marx, the political philosopher and the LCC, London's greatest public servant.

Cross Prince of Wales Road and follow Haverstock Hill back to red buses and trains at Chalk Farm Station.

Oak Village to Queen's Crescent
Circular walk from Gospel Oak Station
For modern map see back cover

Alight at Gospel Oak station (p 102), served by Silverlink trains, or at a bus stop nearby. On this walk we see what remains of the 19th-century development of the fields of Gospel Oak and also assess whether Camden Council's 'scheme of good intentions' to redevelop the area in the 1960s and 1970s has been a success.

Leaving the station, walk right and pause near the crossing in **MANSFIELD ROAD** (p 102). The road was created as early as 1806 on the line of a footpath from South End Green, Hampstead to Highgate Road. Its south side is the northern boundary of the Southampton estate and also of the two Gospel Oak fields that stretched westwards to Southampton Road. In the terrier attached to the 1804 parish map they are listed as leased to the local farmer Richard Mortimer, who was also surveyor of highways and an overseer of the Manor of Tottenhall.

In 1806 the Gospel Oak fields were bought from George Ferdinand Fitzroy, 2nd Baron Southampton, by the Irish peer Cornelius O'Callaghan, 1st Viscount

ROUTE **5**

Lismore (1775-1857). Forty years later they were sold on as building land, after litigation in the Court of Chancery between the Viscount and a Mr Hamilton. This was shortly after Lismore had produced a speculative plan showing semi-detached villas built on plots of 110ft by 50ft covering the whole area. Within a few years two parallel short north-south roads were built at right angles to Mansfield Road and the development of **OAK VILLAGE** (opposite) began, though on considerably smaller plots. This *street* name was evidently derived from their proximity to the site of the famous Gospel Oak (p 76). Early ratebooks recorded the roads as Gospel Oak Village.

Look across Mansfield Road to your left and you will see the entrance to **Nos. 1-8**, while across to your right is another turning leading to **Nos.15-21**. The Old Oak pub and the houses to its right were at first included in the numbering of Oak Village, as Nos.9-14, but were subsequently renumbered as part of Mansfield Road.

Cross over to them by the pedestrian crossing, turn right and then left to pass Nos.15-21. The houses are small, pleasing early-Victorian villas with stuccoed ground floors. They are depicted as semi-detached on the 1869 OS map but have seen much infill over the years. In the 1870s **No.18** was the home of the building materials contractor John Hibbitt, who had a yard in Lamble Street (p 87).

Letters to the press in 1867 complain of rubbish tipping, puddles of dirty water, dead dogs, and children playing in the street, and of "the dank pot-holed state" of the roadway at the back of Oak Village. Residents are concerned that "vehicles can only approach our dwellings by a long and roundabout detour … we are completely isolated from the civilised world in wet weather"; and furthermore that "the poor of Agar Town [swept away by the Midland Railway on the approach to its St Pancras terminus] are crowding, and lowering the character of, the once-promising locality". The railway's own employees later colonised the Village. Booth in 1898 noted that, given its proximity to the railway, there were "many Midland men here".

Opposite **No.17** is another turning that leads to a third, east-west section of the streets named Oak Village which is sometimes called Long Oak Village. The houses here were built slightly later, but before 1860, although curiously they are not shown on the 1862 Stanford map. The well-maintained houses are arranged in twos, their front doors now set back in the joins between each pair, although it is probable that the houses were at first built as semis, with side entrances. None is Listed; individually they lack architectural interest, but the appearance of the whole is attractive.

In the mid-1970s **No.42** was the marital home of the Labour politician Tessa Jowell, currently Secretary of State for Culture, Media and Sport. During the storm of 14 August 1975, the house was badly hit by flooding, as was much of this part of Gospel Oak. The rainfall (6.72 in) had been the highest since the Hampstead Scientific Society began records in 1910. Then Chair of the Camden Council's Social Services Committee, Tessa Jowell led the massive relief operation, which was however hampered by a lack of co-ordination between departments, as was admitted by Camden Council in October that year. One 90-year-old occupant, a Mrs Knight and her husband, had sought refuge on the first floor until the waters subsided. Neighbours on rubber dinghies delivered tea to them in flasks handed through the bedroom window. To prevent further flooding, the Thames Water Authority began work in 1986 on a 6,600-ft relief tunnel under Parliament Hill Fields.

The sculptor and painter Frederick Tatham (1805-78) was living at **No.45** in 1874. His marble bust of his father, the architect and designer Charles Tatham, stands in Trinity Hospital, Greenwich. In his youth Frederick had been a close friend and follower of William Blake, whose widow Catherine moved in to Tatham's house in Lisson Grove as a housekeeper. When she died in 1831, he inherited much of Blake's work and many of his plates. He is said to have later burned several of them in a fit of religious ardour; he had become an Irvingite, one of many fundamentalist movements of the 19th century, and was rigorously opposed to any work smacking of blasphemy.

Intersecting at the west end of the road (after **No.37** on the left), is **JULIA STREET**. It has only four houses, built in 1859 by John Furnell, one of a number of small-scale developers active in Gospel Oak. He leased No.51 Oak Village with Joseph Langham Dale, gentleman, of the County of Middlesex. As we shall see later, Dale is a name that occurs more than once in the history of Gospel Oak. This particular lease was for 88 years, a common term in this area. The origin of the street name is a mystery. Although Bebbington speculates that Julia might have been Furnell's wife or daughter, no 'Julia Furnell' appears in any contemporary census return either here or elsewhere. In 1861, John's wife is strangely missing, and his sister Emma is apparently in charge of his six children, none of whom is called Julia. The family lived at **No.4**, which at that time was No.1A Arthur Grove.

Beyond a slight kink in the road we reach **ELAINE GROVE**, as Arthur Grove was renamed in 1876. A notice in *The Times* on 5 June 1876 mentions the renaming and that the Grove's "irregularly numbered houses" were being re-numbered. The street may have originally been named in honour of Prince Arthur, Queen Victoria's third son (b.1850). The Grove's present name could have been inspired by Arthurian legend or one of Tennyson's poems. Elaine Grove is another street of small semi-detached early Victorian houses. Booth in 1898 described them as home to the "decent working class; 2 families to a house generally".

In the 1960s the residents of the three streets we have just walked through were very concerned when plans were unveiled to demolish all these properties as part of a comprehensive redevelopment plan for Gospel Oak. Many owned their homes and campaigned to retain them. They succeeded partly because they were able to show that no additional homes would be provided in the redevelopment plans. Elaine Grove, however, lost buildings at the west end: on the north side Nos.1-8, of which the first two were shops, and on the south side the pub, the Duke of Cornwall. Named as a compliment to the future Edward VII, this imposing pub with three street frontages stood on the corner of Lismore Circus (at No.11).

Now, turn left into the spacious walking area known as **Heriot Place**, which lies slightly to the east of a short Victorian street commemorating Joseph Jennings Heriot, a retired Kentish Town ironmonger. The street led from Mansfield Road to Lismore Circus and the houses on its western side were pulled down in the redevelopment of the area during the late 1960s. Opposite is the end of **Ludham**, which faces Waxham (p 103) across private gardens. Like most blocks hereabouts, Ludham takes its name from a village in Norfolk. The new open space of Heriot Place is provided with low concrete seating.

We enter **LISMORE CIRCUS**. Now somewhat forlorn, the Circus was the focus of the plans made by Viscount Lismore around 1845 for a spacious suburb of semi-detached villas But he sold off the land in small plots that attracted buyers of small means, who built, when they could afford to do so, as many mean houses as possible along the roads radiating from the Circus. These were painfully slow to arrive. By 1853 only about a dozen west of Oak Village had been built, together with "a beershop on the corner" said to have been "the favourite resort of navvies and quarrelsome shoemakers".

The area was still little better than a poorly regulated building site when the Midland's surveyors arrived in 1866. They asked the celebrated architect Sir William Tite for an opinion. "The properties at Gospel Oak", he said, "are humble. I do not mean to say that they are to be disregarded because they are humble, but they are very humble; some of them are very inferior, ill-built and wretched." The district was still unpaved, unlit and unhealthy. A petition to the Privy Council

Office from the inhabitants in 1859 had warned of the dangers "created by the division of the water from the Fleet Ditch" in its passage through Gospel Oak Fields. "Ponds are formed for brickmaking purposes ... and are receptacles for vast quantities of poisonous matter. Ice is taken from these ponds during the winter months for sale in the Metropolis...." The brickfields were owned by George Bassett, Lord Southampton's agent.

The Circus itself was still, in 1867, a "mud island", Lismore having failed to provide any support for its upkeep. It is even doubtful whether he ever conveyed the Circus land to anyone, which led to later disputes as to who was responsible. Residents in 1869 asked the Vestry to take it over, complaining of the disgraceful condition of the surrounding roads and loneliness of the locality. Hampstead and Kentish Town were the nearest places to board a coach. It was not until 1880 that horse-drawn trams began their journeys along Southampton Road and Malden Road into central London.

The protest resulted in the central garden being laid out in 1870-71, but there were disagreements over who could use it. For a short time in 1890 it was opened to the public, but residents complained of noise made by children. In 1899 the gardens were remade and the public again admitted. By this time, Lismore Circus was a thriving local shopping area, now remembered fondly by older people [25].

All the properties in Lismore Circus were demolished in the 1960s as part of the comprehensive redevelopment of Gospel Oak. Plans drawn up by Armstrong and MacManus for St Pancras Council in 1962 included a new shopping centre arranged in a crescent around the garden, but the new Camden Council which came into being in 1965 abandoned this scheme. A tower block, a family health centre, a football practice pitch and a few shops were built approximately around the periphery but without any attempt to make them cohere. Camden Council recently provided funds to refurbish the garden, but its forlorn air remains, since the Circus itself is no longer either a residential or a shopping area.

In the 19th century Henry Slack, "King of Donkey Drivers" lived at No.13.

Henry Slack has got a son
Can't he make the donkeys run!

25   Haverstock Hill Station and the former Railway Tavern on Lismore Circus c. 1900

Before committing suicide at the age of 42 by drowning in Highgate Ponds, Slack had run a fishbone into his hand and poisoned it, ending up in St Bartholomew's Hospital.

Walking clockwise around the Circus, we pass the end of **LAMBLE STREET**. This was one of seven roads leading from the Circus like the spokes of the wheel. It was originally Circus Road East but was renamed in 1887 after the builder and Vestryman Samuel Richard Lamble. On the south side stood the Lamble Street Hall, at first a mission hall of the London City Mission, which was taken over in 1923 by Primitive Methodists previously in Grafton Road (p 51); they remained here until they joined the Gospel Oak Methodist Church in 1956. The houses on the north side were constructed by 1868. Thirty years later, according to Booth, they had become "rather rough". They were pulled down and replaced, in 1978, by the present row of white town houses with covered car ports, each with a roof garden and a small back garden. The architects were G Benson and A Forsyth of Camden; the former lived locally. Facing these town houses is the earlier block of maisonettes, **Nos.24–39**.

A footpath leads off to the back of this development, but we walk through the small woodland garden, created with funds from Camden Council, that lies alongside. A plaque records that the garden is looked after by a group of volunteers, who have chosen trees and plants that attract birds and insects to the area. In Spring the ground is covered with wild flowers. This was once the site of a short cul-de-sac called Lismore Gardens, which ended at the railway line. It contained the stonemason's yard and Lismore Studios of "marble merchants" W T Stevenson & Co., a firm established in 1947 that made garden ornaments using "natural stone from London's Historic Blitzed Buildings". At the end of the garden turn right to regain **LISMORE CIRCUS**.

Continue round the Circus, crossing the Midland main line where it burrows beneath the central gardens; a brick wall surmounted by a metal fence lies above the tunnel entrance. The railway cutting to your left follows the line of an eastward extension of Lismore Road (p 88) that was lost to the railway while still on the drawing-board; before that it had been a footpath that ran southeast from Hampstead across the fields to Kentish Town. Next cross the end of a walkway that was once the northern tip of Allcroft Road (p 89), and pass Bacton High Rise flats. These stand on the site of No.1 Lismore Circus, *alias* Ventnor House, which in 1874 housed 'Christian Meeting Rooms' and a decade later had become the Oak Village Gospel Hall. The group of nonconformists who ran this mission from 1875 were later involved in the building of the Methodist Church in Agincourt Road, Hampstead.

The low ramp a little farther on marks the spot where Haverstock Road (p 14) debouched into the Circus. The **Gospel Oak Community Health Clinic** stands over to our left. By 1878 the corner site on the Circus was taken by the Wheatsheaf pub, where Dr Hardwicke and others held public inquests. The pub was demolished with the rest of the buildings in Lismore Circus in the 1960s, bringing to an end its regular music nights that were notable for the duets of landlord Phil Hood on trumpet and Wally Fawkes on clarinet. During WWII a local ARP post was situated in the garden. This area suffered much bomb damage in WWII. Several decades later, local resident Michael Palin, *Monty Python* star turned TV globetrotter, ceremonially planted an oak tree here in an attempt to replace the long-lost Gospel Oak, but the tree has not survived.

Looking over towards the garden you will see that one of the paths from the centre of Lismore Circus leads to where we are standing. Fig **[25]** shows Haverstock Hill train station as it appeared from this position in the 19th and early 20th centuries, on the corner of the Circus with Rochford Street (p 88). Keith Scholey wrote in *The Railways of Camden* that "the buildings had the ornate bargeboards more commonly seen on the Midland's country stations: clearly, a special effort was made for what was then a better quality neighbourhood". One can take a more cynical view. The Midland Railway wished to assuage the fears of residents who, when the station opened in 1868, began to realise that the new railway would have a disastrous effect on the value of local properties. The naming of the station was not totally perverse: although we are here over half a mile from the eponymous thoroughfare, the whole of the area to the east of it was long known as 'Haverstock Hill'. Used by the less affluent to take advantage of cheap late-night shopping for perishable goods in local shops, the station closed in 1916, a victim (like the Midland's station in Camden Road) of competition from the trams. It was let as a warehouse before it was destroyed by fire in the 1960s.

Note the side road on the left of **[25]**. This was Circus Road, begun in the early 1850s. In the 1870s the Haverstock Rooms, next to the Rose Laundry a little way along on the north side, were the headquarters of the Plymouth Brethren, one of many religious sects which moved into the new neighbourhood to provide spiritual and practical support. By the 1930s the Rose Laundry had become the premises of the Percy Metal Co. Also in Circus Road, at No.3, was the Gospel Oak National Schools for girls and infants, not to be confused with the earlier Birkbeck School in the road, which had given way to the railway. Circus Road was renamed in April 1887; at first called Wetenhall

Street, after William Wettenhall who at the time was a Vestryman, a member of the Metropolitan Board of Works and landlord of the Lord Southampton pub (p 75), but by 1888 it had been named Rochford Street, for reasons unknown. On his poverty map of 1889 Booth labelled it purple ("some comfortable, others poor") and there was a common lodging house in the street. In 1918 the Sunlight and Remedial Exercise Clinic was started at No.14 Rochford Street; it survived on voluntary contributions into the mid-1930s and was attended by children of the nearby day nursery in Gospel Oak Grove. The modern **Gospel Oak Nursery Centre** now lies off Lismore Circus, and was expanded in 2002-03. The rump of the street remains as a short turning out of Southampton Road over to the west, known as **NEW ROCHFORD STREET**.

Opposite the Brethren's hall stood a pub, the King Harold. Here Rochford Street was bisected by Gospel Oak Grove, a dog-leg street whose southern half was known as Harold Street till 1879. It was then combined with earlier-built Grove Cottages to the north, where the road bridged the Midland railway. An early Sanitary Committee report noted that eleven houses in Gospel Oak Grove were without sewers or cesspools; "the privy drainage goes on the surface of the land". Also in the road was the piano factory

of G Thomas, badly damaged by fire in 1884. By 1898 Booth recorded that Gospel Oak Grove was a working-class street, the children "well clad and shod; fairly clean".

On the right-hand side of **[25]** (p 86), next to the station, is a building that remained here until the area was redeveloped. It was initially a public house, listed in 1874 as the Railway Tavern. A decade later it had become a British Working Men's Club and Institute. This was still thriving before WWII, as the North St Pancras Working Men's Club.

Lismore Road entered the Circus at this point, approaching diagonally from the corner of Southampton and Mansfield Roads. In Hope Cottage, Lismore Road, the mechanical and chemical engineer Herbert Alfred Humphrey (1868–1951) was born, a son of the accountant to the Metropolitan Board of Works. A consulting engineer, he invented the Humphrey gas pump, which overcame many problems of earlier types. After WWI he became consulting engineer and director of a new chemical engineering company at Billingham, subsequently home to Imperial Chemical Industries (ICI) on its formation in 1926. Humphrey helped construct the 40,000 kW electric power station there, which was well in advance of central station design at the time.

Lismore Road had mainly 3-storey houses, which in 1898 Booth noted were "respectable", the inhabitants giving "little trouble". At its junction with Gospel Oak Grove (see above) stood a further pub, the Prince Alfred, named after Victoria's second son. At Nos.37-39 an early cinema, the Lismore, operated briefly from 1914. Converted out of two adjoining eating-places, and run by a James Kerrison, it somehow seated 500. After the picture-house closed in 1917, the premises became the Lucania Temperance Billiard Hall. Before its eventual demolition, Lismore Road enjoyed two last moments of glory, serving as a film-set in the movie *Georgie Girl* (1966), starring Rita Tushingham and Lynn Redgrave. The road played the role of Carnaby Street, its run-down shop fronts disguised as trendy boutiques. A year later, it was again used for location shots, in the filming of *Smashing Time*, which featured the same two actresses.

Complete the circuit of the Circus by passing the enclosed football practice area. Beyond is Ludham. On the ground floor are a few useful shops, and the Ludham and Waxham Tenants' and Residents' Association Hall. Retrace your steps and leave the Circus by taking the footpath with 22-storey **Bacton High Rise** on your right. The block, surmounted by a forest of mobile-phone masts, takes its name from a Norfolk village. Bacton and the buildings to the west as far as Southampton Road were built to a higher density than the rest of Gospel Oak by Armstrong and MacManus in the 1960s. Tenants moved in in 1967.

We shall follow the Estate on our right as we walk along **WELLESLEY ROAD**. Known at first as Church Road, in 1866 it was renamed Allcroft Road, after the benefactor of St Martin's church (p 94). It retained this name until the area was redeveloped a century later, when the street became part of Wellesley Road, which originally ran further south. Wellesley is the family name of the Duke of Wellington (1769-1852). The only Victorian properties to remain are those on the left, which now bear Wellesley Road numbers. The site on your left was occupied from 1864 by the Gospel Oak Schools, displaced from Circus Road by the Midland Railway after only a couple of years. These were among the ten Birkbeck schools opened by the philanthropist and educator William Ellis (1880-1881) in honour of the pioneer educator George Birkbeck (1776-1841). The mixed establishment had nearly 800 pupils. In 1887 it became the William Ellis Endowed School and in 1937 moved to Highgate Road. During WWII this building housed a gas mask depot and ambulance garage, one of four Civil Defence depots in St Pancras. Gospel Oak suffered quite badly from bomb damage, with Allcroft Road an early casualty. On 8 September 1940, the first day of raids on St Pancras, a high-explosive bomb fell close to the depot, shattering an Anderson shelter and killing several shelterers. The

Prime Minister's wife, Mrs Clementine Churchill, visiting the depot on 30 September 1941, was impressed by the workshop where the men made children's toys out of timber salvaged from bombed premises. The Scout 'hut', the first brick-built building on the left, was erected in 1897, as can be seen from the carved numerals in the gable. The building today is the HQ of the St Pancras Scout Group, and is also used by the Queen's Crescent Hawks Youth Club run by Gospel Oak Action Link.

Next door, at **No.117**, part of the old Victorian buildings is used as a meeting hall by the tenants of the Wendling Estate. **No.115** beyond is post-WWII and is used by the local housing and social services departments. Also based here is the GO Partnership, an organisation that is dedicated to improving the lives of people in Gospel Oak and the surrounding area. On the right, at the foot of Bacton High Rise, is a pleasant garden containing drought-resistant plants in the popular style introduced by Beth Chatto.

Creepers and trees hanging over the wall of the next property ahead on our left hide the house and garden of the new Vicarage. If you are passing in late summer or early autumn look up into the canopy of foliage above the pavement and admire bunches of grapes.

Turn left into **VICARS ROAD**, which was developed in 1866. Its name, Vicar's

Road, was approved in the same year, and so, with or without the apostrophe, it has always been known. The labels "Vicar Street" on the 1868 parish map and "Vicarage Road" on the OS map of 1894 were erroneous. Back gardens of the houses on the north side were on the boundary of the 5-acre Gospel Oak Field and of the Fourteen Acre Field, the Church Lands field owned by St Pancras church.

Soon we reach the front entrance to the present St Martin's Vicarage, at **No.26** (officially No.113 Wellesley Road). The parish is now known as the united parish of St Martin with St Andrew, amalgamated in 1953. We shall pass the site of demolished St Andrew's in Malden Road later in this walk (p 94). The vicarage is housed in a maisonette built in the early 1970s, as were the 18 flats of the World of Property Housing Trust at **No.24**. The buildings replaced the large vicarage that was contemporary with the church opposite.

The next building on this north side, erected in 1904, is **St Martin's Hall** (its name inscribed on the façade). Constructed of Kentish ragstone like the church, it housed the Sunday school. By this date, St Martin's parochial day school – provided by the patron of the church, J D Allcroft, which had a "neat and excellently equipped schoolroom" – had closed. The building was sold in the 1980s and since 1993 has been occupied by a primary and nursery school, delightfully

named *L'Île aux enfants*. This teaches the French curriculum to both French expatriate and local children.

Adjacent to the hall, at **No.20**, is the former verger's house. The flowers growing in pots and boxes against the side wall lighten up the dark alley that separate the two buildings. Beyond No.20 the rest of the north side of Vicars Road is now covered by post-WWII warehousing. In the 1870s No.12 was the base for a school run by Mrs E Lamble, possibly related to Samuel Lamble (p 87).

Cross the road and take a look at the two semi-detached houses at the corner. **No.53**, on the right, originally No.21, has elegant, bulbous iron railings decorating the first-floor balcony. It was built with the church as the vicar's glebe house, which protected it during redevelopment of the area in the 1960s. The adjoining house (**No.51**) also survived, as by 1974 Camden Council had abandoned its commitment to bulldozing. Sid Rawl, nationally recognised as a leader of the squatter movement in the 1970s, took over No.51 at this time and within days, the vicar was astounded to learn, had arranged for water, heating and a telephone to be connected. He moved on to other accommodation (provided by Camden Council) when he was later asked to do so. The Council allowed many groups of people to have short-term housing leases on the understanding that they would move out when the house was

required for redevelopment.

No.53 abuts the garden of **St Martin's Church**. Walk to the entrance to the church at the north door. Consecrated in 1865, it was built to a design by Edward Buckton Lamb [26]. Nikolaus Pevsner, in 1952, dubbed St Martin's "the craziest Victorian church in London". Lamb has been the butt of much criticism, but Pevsner's description has done nothing but good in keeping the building in the sights of church architecture buffs. Simon Jenkins included St Martin's in his book of 1000 best churches, and it is now Grade I Listed. The church historian Basil Clark writes "this is a church that is not easy to describe: it must be seen". So take his advice and visit on a Sunday (the church is also sometimes open on a Tuesday morning). A recently published illustrated history is available. The magnificent hammerbeam roof alone makes the visit worthwhile. In the north transept hangs the wooden war memorial calvary from old St Andrew's Church (p 94), together with that of St Martin's. Outside, the inscriptions in Gothic text around the church tower read "Praise the lord O my soul" and "Forget not all his benefits who forgiveth all thine iniquities".

The church was funded by the wealthy glove manufacturer John Derby Allcroft of Stokesay Court, Shropshire, whose monogram is on the outside south wall of the nave. He gave about £30,000 for

the church and another £15,000 for the
vicarage, Sunday schools and Mission Hall.
Lamb's own monogram is engraved on the
north wall of the nave inside the church. A
new hall and church offices were converted
in 1985 by Pickard and Palmer from 1930s
additions.

A local newspaper article in 1904 stated
that before the church was built some
people thought that "the local population
was too poor to support a chapel". He
went on to say "but if the neighbourhood
is poor in money matters it is passing rich
in the number of its splendid spiritually-
upright agencies".

Return to the corner of **WELLESLEY
ROAD** and turn left. Over to the right are
the flats (**Nos.196-218**) of **Bacton Low
Rise**. On your left, past the church, runs
a pleasant tree-lined footpath roughly on
the line of the old Dale Road, which ran
parallel to Vicars Road; we shall visit its
short eastern arm later.

Ahead lies the Queen's Crescent
North Estate, another comprehensive
redevelopment of the 1960s, in which
several streets were wholly destroyed and
the street pattern was radically altered. To
your left, south of former Dale Road and

ROUTE **5**

running east to join Grafton Road (p 97), was Hanover Street. Here was the childhood home of Wally Whyton (1929-1997), later leader of the Vipers skiffle group, and then a children's entertainer, a mainstay of children's programmes in the early years of ITV. Older readers may recall his appearances in *Small Time*, in which he provided the voice of the glove-puppet owl, Ollie Beak. In 1938 Hanover Street became Gilden Road, in a probably arbitrary renaming by the LCC. (Bebbington

suggests that 'Gilden' relates to a field where geldings were grazed, but there is no evidence of such land use hereabouts.)

The footpath directly ahead runs in front of **Wellesley** flats (**Nos.2-104**), which we meet again later. The path follows roughly the line of a street known as Langford Road until 1879, when it was renumbered as a southward extension of Allcroft Road (p 89).

West of it ran Langford Mews, accessed through a covered entry at No.90 Allcroft

Road. In 1882 the mews was taken over by the Sainsbury family, who by then already had two shops in nearby Queen's Crescent (p 44). They turned a private house in the mews into offices and accommodation for their foreman. Three of the four stables became warehouses for butter, cheese and eggs, and two bacon-smoking ovens were installed on the site [27]. The Sainsburys left in 1891. After WWII two blocks of pre-fabricated houses were built at the north end of the Mews, in a space cleared of badly bombed housing.

Ignoring the path ahead, follow the bend in the road as it swings to the right to reach the alignment of the *original* Wellesley Road, whose name was approved in 1867, and which once ran south from here to meet Queen's Crescent. In the 1960s redevelopment, the road was diverted to run north-eastward, forming the route we have just followed, and absorbing the north end of Allcroft Road.

Continue along present-day Wellesley Road to where it bends further to the right, into its surviving original north end. Here on the right, for about a century, stood the Prince of Wales pub. On your left is a group of red-brick buildings that house the **Wellesley Road Home for Older People**, opened in 1974 for 48 permanent residents.

27 Langford Mews: Sainsbury's warehouses and bacon-smoking ovens (company price card c.1885, Sainsbury's Archive)

28 'The Castle' at No.15 Oakfield Crescent, briefly the 'ridiculous' home of Jerome K Jerome

There was great joy on 22 February 2001 after a High Court decision against the Council allowed the home to remain open.

Opposite, the long block of flats (**Nos.153-175 Bacton Low Rise**) covers the entrance to former Oakfield Crescent, which disappeared under the new development. The road – built up by 1860 – was lined with terraced houses, but No.15 stood out. Castellated and stepped back, it was known as The Castle. It was once briefly the home of Jerome K Jerome (1859-1927). Born in Walsall, Jerome was brought up in Poplar, where his parents had settled, and where his father, a failed lay preacher and coalmine owner, had set himself up as an ironmonger. Both his parents died when he was a teenager and he took a job as a railway clerk at Euston Station. He frequently changed lodgings in an attempt to relieve his loneliness. Among his addresses was The Castle **[28]**, "a ridiculous little house off Malden Road", as he wrote in his memoirs. "I had the top chamber in the tower. For some things it was convenient. I could lie in bed in the centre of the room and reach everything I wanted." Just when he lived in Oakfield Crescent is not clear, but he claimed to have been "lodging off the Malden Road" when the [Park] Theatre in Camden Town burned down [11 September 1881], and to have been "awakened by the glare upon [his] window." Later, after successive spells as a schoolmaster, reporter, actor and journalist, Jerome embarked on a literary career. His most famous work, *Three Men in a Boat*, was published in 1889. For some years he was co-editor of *The Idler* magazine. In 1893 he started his own twopenny magazine called *The Weekly*, serialising Robert Louis Stevenson's *Ebb Tide*. But this enterprise ended in a lawsuit. His most famous play is a modern morality tale called *The Passing of the Third Floor Back*, which was produced in 1908.

Next we come to an empty site used for private parking once occupied by Nos.49-55 Wellesley Road before we reach the corner of **HAVERSTOCK ROAD**. Named after Haverstock Hill, its houses were assigned numbers in 1869. It originally led into Lismore Circus, but is now a cul-de-sac with its northern end reduced to a service road leading to the garages of the flats on either side, completed in 1967.

Cross the end of the road and walk up the incline, ahead and to the right, gaining a higher level area at the south end of the **Wendling** Estate, named after another Norfolk village. Walk through the barriers and up a further ramp, passing **Prince**

Arthur House on the left. All the buildings here are by Armstrong and MacManus, "a bewildering maze of small courts" (Pevsner), built from the early 1960s.

Veer to the left and walk to the spiral staircase that stands in the gap between two buildings. Descend the few steps that lead to a wide pavement on the corner of Southampton Road and Malden Road, opposite the church of St Dominic's (p 75). The land here was sold by Lord Southampton at auction on 24 June 1840. We are standing on Lot 84 which had a frontage of 187ft on what became Southampton Road and 173 ft on what became Malden Road, and was sold for £50.

We turn left into **MALDEN ROAD** (p 67), which was not officially assigned house numbers until 1863. This was before most of this northern end of the east side was built up. The remaining houses were completed by 1867 and renumbered. These substantial houses were built close to the roadway. On the corner stood Nos.190-92, a draper's and tailor's established in the 1860s by John Burnard. He also ran a local post office. The north end of Malden Road was classed as 'fairly comfortable' on Booth's poverty maps but, like most of Gospel Oak, later became a mixed area.

Further down we reach the 1960s buildings called **St Stephen's Close**, oddly named, in September 1959, since

they were built on the site of the Victorian church of St Andrew. St Andrew's was built in 1866 at a cost of £4,500 to a Gothic design by the architect Charles Hayward [29]. It could seat 840, with 440 seats classed as free to encourage poorer inhabitants to attend. Indeed, a working men's committee had agitated from 1856 to 1863 for the church to be built and, perhaps inspired by Samuel Smiles' *Self Help*, had themselves collected funds for a new church and school. The vicarage was some distance away at No.147 Haverstock Hill. The church flourished for nearly a century. It was closed in 1953, but not without a fervent appeal to the High Court. In the same year the parish was joined with St Martin's, and St Andrew's was subsequently demolished.

It had stood on the corner of L-shaped Piercefield Street (wrongly marked as "Piersfield Street" on the 1869 OS map) whose southern arm once joined Malden Road at this point. James Parker Pierce, a retired Soho jeweller, owned the small field on which the street was built. Piercefield Terrace was the early name of an adjacent range of houses facing Southampton Road. Booth, in 1898, considered Piercefield Street to be "rather rough". No.23, on its northeast corner, successively housed a Victorian mineral-water works run by Herbert Hearn and his family, and later (until after WWII) the piano factory of Monington and Weston.

29 St Andrew's, Malden Road (*The Builder*, 14 Sep 1867)

Very shortly, we pass the southern end of **Wendling** (**Nos.49-57**) and cross Haverstock Road (p 94). On the far corner is the **Westport Inn**, which caters for a largely Irish clientele – with an emerald-green fascia and named after the County Mayo resort. It was originally built in the late 1850s and called the Gipsy [sic] Queen, which name it retained until 1974. The pub was rebuilt in the 1930s, its ground-floor exterior faced in dark glazed tiles.

Next come two original terraced houses, which at first formed part of a short Gipsey [sic] Terrace, of which the Gipsy Queen was No.1. **No.164** is a branch of Levertons (p 33). They took over the shop in 1992 from another firm of undertakers called Madley's, who were established in Malden Road in 1874 on the corner with Wellesley Place (see below). An early occupant of **No.162** was the Haverstock Hill and Malden Road Provident Dispensary, from 1865 until 1881, when it moved to No.132. It had three categories of members: free, honorary and charitable, this last being for those who were too poor to pay the twopence (1p) a week family contribution made by 'free' members. After WWII, No.162 was a barber shop until the Sharp family moved here in 1964 from their previous shop in Weedington Road, where they had sold wireless equipment and serviced the accumulators of wireless sets of the many local people whose homes lacked electricity. In Malden Road they turned

ROUTE **5**

95

their love of fishing into their livelihood. Bob Sharp continues to sell goods required by local anglers and his window display is quirky. It is the only fishing tackle shop still open in this area, the nearby shop run by Harry Bowditch in the 1960s having closed.

The side of No.162 now overlooks the forecourt of the **Court Garage**. On this large site the St Andrew's National School was opened shortly after the church was completed in 1866; for a few years previously its building had functioned as a temporary church and school. The National School had separate departments for boys and girls, with an infants' school behind the latter, but it could not compete with the local Board school and closed in 1909. The following year, the Gem Picture Hall, possibly the earliest cinema in Kentish Town, opened on the site. In 1919 it became the Doric Picture Theatre and in 1922 was briefly known as the Malden Picture Hall before being renamed again as the Court. The cinema had only 460 seats but despite much local competition attracted a very loyal audience. The Court remained open until 1958, by which time it was affectionately known as the "flea-pit": people can still remember the usherettes spraying pesticide to kill the bugs and flies. The site was taken over by the present service station, which no longer sells petrol.

Beyond the garage forecourt is a small road that now leads into the garage. This is all that remains of Wellesley Place which once led to Wellesley Road, entering it opposite the Prince of Wales Tavern; the short street was initially called, rather grandly, Prince of Wales Avenue.

Continue past the bus stop. On your left is a large **open space**, with the character of an urban park, although from this angle the enclosed sports arenas are more prominent. A board gives information about the various activities of the sports club that meets here at weekends. The area between Malden Road and Grafton Road was cleared of its slum-like dwellings as part of the Queen's Crescent North regeneration of the late 1960s, the residents moving out in the early 1970s.

Facing us on the far side of the green is the long line of flats that were built with three other long blocks, parallel and to the east, to house those who had lost their homes in the clearance. The first block is Wellesley, which we saw earlier. We shall consider the history of the development further when we reach this and the other blocks later (p 97).

Proceed along Malden Road. Approaching from the right is Grafton Terrace (p 79), which once continued on this side to meet old Wellesley Road. Originally called Huckle Street, this short continuation disappeared during the 1960s. The Haverstock Hill and Malden Road Provident Dispensary (p 95) occupied its second home at former No.132 Malden Road, just beyond Grafton Terrace, from 1881 until WWI.

A little further on, we cross **GILDEN CRESCENT**, laid out in the 1960s and named after demolished Gilden Road (p 92). On the left is the new development of flats, **Nos.6-61**, some with attractive planting. The expanse of modern yellow brick on the building at the bend on the right (**No.3**) masks the fact that the core of the building is mid-Victorian. It used to front Wellesley Road, whose southern end was incorporated into Gilden Crescent.

Continue along **MALDEN ROAD**. **Nos.110-118** were built in the late 1850s as part of Howell Terrace, which stretched as far as former No.128. Gleaming new state-of-the-art bicycles are stacked up outside the well-known cycle shop **Simpsons** at Nos.114-116. This was taken over in 1972 by Brian Simpson (d.2003), who had worked for the previous owners Howard Clark since leaving school shortly after WWII. His widow and two sons continue to run the shop as a family firm.

We turn the corner into Queen's Crescent (see Route 2), taking a close look at the daily market, which is at its most lively on Saturdays, when it is difficult to understand why the market has trouble surviving. Continue past the southern end of Gilden Crescent (where Wellesley Road once began) to the next turning left, a fragment of old Allcroft Road that is the western arm of a new service road called

ASHDOWN CRESCENT. Emerging from the left at the next turning (ahead) is its eastern arm, all that remains of Ashdown Street, from which the new Crescent borrowed its name. Ashdown Street, which ran north to join Gilden Road (p 92), was named after Edwin Ashdown, of Malden Crescent, who owned the land on which it was built.

Ascend the incline that leads on your left to the **Queen's Crescent Community Centre**, one of the focal buildings in the area. Four facilities, including the Ashdown Youth Centre and Maitland Park Gym, are managed from these premises. The first centre on this site was opened in 1978. It flourished at first, with stand-up comics providing live entertainment, but it degenerated into a drinking club. By the late 1980s it was used solely as a lunchtime dining club, supported by Inter-Action (p 54). In 1999 a grant from the GO Partnership (p 89) enabled it to become the lively community centre it is today. It provides a wide range of activities for people of all ages, interests and backgrounds. On Fridays it houses many Muslim worshippers overflowing from the nearby mosque (p 45).

Walk on towards the south end of Wellesley, the long block of flats built roughly on the line of the east side of vanished Allcroft Road, whose northern end we encountered earlier. The Queen's Crescent North development was probably the most ambitious of Camden Council's schemes and is one of their most successful. The work was carried out by Frederick MacManus and Partners from 1972 to 1979. On this west side of the long 4-storey building, access is from flights of steps placed at regular intervals; there are no raised walkways on this Estate. A slip road from the north provides entry to a private underground car park.

Bear right, taking the footpath that runs along the south side of the development and admire the long, well laid out garden at the rear of the block. Through the foliage at the far end you can see the tower of St Martin's and Bacton High Rise. Backing on to the garden on the right is another long block, with its entrances in Weedington Road. The garden and flats stand roughly on the line of former Ashdown Street.

Continue walking, past the barrier that prevents access by cars, and reach the northern end of **WEEDINGTON ROAD** (p 44), the only road in this area remaining from the original Victorian development but whose houses have been replaced by the long blocks at **Nos.131-319** (whose backs we have just seen) and on the opposite side **Nos.172-376**. The latter replaced the former Carlton Cottages, an early development shown on the 1860 map, renumbered three years later as part of a much longer Weedington Road. So closely spaced were the parallel north-south streets hereabouts that there were no houses on the west side, which was lined only by the small back yards of dwellings in Ashdown Street, while the houses on Weedington Road's east side were back-to-back with those on the west side of Carlton Street, the next street eastward. Booth noted in 1898 that the 3-storey houses were "very thickly populated", and had a poor reputation, but he added that there were "no broken windows or open doors". Cross the road and continue ahead on the narrower footpath to reach another long rear garden, laid out quite differently but also well planted. The garden lies along the line of Carlton (later Carltoun) Street, whose likewise demolished southern end is referred to in Route 2 (p 45).

The path ends in **GRAFTON ROAD** by the side of **Nos.161-349**. Grafton Road (cf. p 50) was called Carlton Road until 1937. This road, like both Carlton Street and Carlton Cottages, was incorrectly labelled as "Calton" on the 1868 parish map. Opposite us stands the **Carlton Primary School**, opened in 1884 and a typical tall London School Board building of the period. It once accommodated 1553 pupils in three departments – boys, girls and infants – but now caters for 400. A gate to the left was the original infants' entrance, with the girls' entrance and old school house ahead.

Look left along the east side of Grafton Road, which still retains its plain-fronted houses, some with clumsy porticoes, built in the 1850s in ranges known initially as Havelock, Spencer and Lansdowne Terraces. This early development stopped at the boundary with the Church Lands' Fourteen Acre Field, but continued in 1858 when the church let the land for the building of Dale Road and Vicars Road (p 89).

Now turn right and walk along to the Mamelon Tower (p 50). Trespassing again into Route 2, we cross the road and walk east along the north side of Queen's Crescent (p 50) past a high school playground wall. By Cresswood Hall bear left into the northern end of **WOODYARD CLOSE** (p 49). Here, stretching northward, was the extensive yard of timber merchant Bignell George Elliot, hence the street name. The northwest corner of the timber yard site once contained an industrial complex comprising four main blocks, and known as the Carlton Works. Its occupants before WWI included Thomas Caslake, a wrought ironworker, and Louis Vaney, a maker of pianos. Long-standing tenants were J W Abbey & Co., manufacturers of 'silicate cotton'. Dating from 1977-81, the homely, suburban-style housing of the modern Close was designed by Camden Council architects Sheila Tribe and Diana Baker. By **No.40**, the last house in the row that faces us ahead, there is a view of the railway viaduct of the elevated North London railway line, which runs behind.

Now walk up the pedestrian route that leads into **CRESSFIELD CLOSE**, another pleasant suburban enclave laid out with small houses, low-rise flats and gardens planned around parking areas, again to the designs of Tribe and Baker. The development follows St Pancras Council's 1964 statement that residents should not suffer the disadvantages of living on roads used by motorists as a through route. As the street name suggests, there were once watercress beds hereabouts, regularly inundated by the River Fleet.

Follow the road as it bends first left then right and eventually, on the right, reaches an old brick wall and an almost hidden door, whose existence is betrayed by an old-fashioned latch. This is the entrance to one of the most delightful attractions for children in London: the **Kentish Town City Farm**. Spare some time to look at the collection of animals and watch the enjoyment of the young volunteers who look after them. Walk to the far end of the farm, where the horses are kept and children can learn to ride. The seat overlooking the sheep is a good place to rest, observing too the constant flow of traffic on the various railway lines that cross the area.

The farm lies on land purchased by the Midland Railway from St Pancras Church in the early 1860s. Here after WWII was the timber yard of Gloster Parquet Company, who shared the site with the garages of S Seth Coach Co. Later in the 1960s the buildings were taken over as short-term housing by Inter-Action (p 54), who used them for an educational project. A garden space was made for the local community, and these early plots are still cultivated. Horses were donated and stables built, and a qualified instructor taught riding. The Talacre project provided goats. In 1974 the site was named the Fun Art Farm, assuming its present name four years later. It was the first City Farm in the country and was soon running an advisory service for communities who wished to start similar projects. It is now run by a local management committee, with an enthusiastic group of young volunteers. Core funding is provided by Camden Council with donations by charities; individual donations are also welcomed. Fund-raising is an ongoing concern and full use is made of Christmas and Easter Fairs and Apple Days.

When you leave, turn right and shortly turn right again into a rural alley that leads into the rump of **DALE ROAD**. Laid out across the Church Lands from 1858 the road once stretched as far west as Allcroft Road. It was probably named after Thomas Dale, the popular vicar of St Pancras from 1846 to 1860 (**[2]**, p 10). He created the St Pancras church extension scheme which, as the population increased, divided the old parish up into 30 smaller ecclesiastical units. Nestling behind trees by the side of the main railway line to our right are **Nos.2-8**, mid-Victorian 3-storey houses, with stucco window surrounds. These houses survived while others further to the east were sacrificed to the Midland Railway.

Look over to the recently restored house on the corner of **GRAFTON ROAD**, **No.242**. This was built as the Mitre pub, named as a compliment to the Bishop of London, and sold to the Midland Railway in the 1860s, which needed it as a place for navvies to slake their thirst when constructing the railway line. Before its recent restoration for residential use, there were six splendid heads of Neptune decorating the building. These are now in private hands. In the immediate post-war years a large pigeon loft was attached to the pub wall facing the railway, at a time when keeping pigeons was still a popular pastime. As recently as 1975, pigeons kept by a Mr Avis drowned in the Oak Village Flood of that year (p 84).

Turn right along Grafton Road. On its opposite side is the northern end of the 1970s Queen's Crescent North Estate we have encircled on our walk. Vicars Road, entering from the left, lost its eastern end to the Midland Railway in the 1860s. Ascend the incline and cross over the bridge spanning the old Midland Railway line. The slip road

on the left, **BARRINGTON CLOSE**, leads into a further Council estate. The roadway follows the line of the original Grafton Road, which led through to Lamble Street, joining it by the mission hall (p 87). Facing the latter, at what was then No.174 Carlton Road, was a pub, the Builder's Arms, which had an entertainment licence. Its landlord in 1874 was Robert W Hunton. A decade later he gave up the licensed trade and took up piano making. He later went into partnership, and No.174 became the piano factory of Messrs. Hunton & Crocker.

Barrington Court is a 10-storey block of small flats designed by Powell and Moya in 1952-54 for St Pancras Council, whose block-naming policy for western Kentish Town (cf. p 45) is reflected in the estate's Somerset village name; later Gospel Oak blocks received their Norfolk names from *Camden* Council. It lies at the western end of the old brickworks (see Kiln Place, below), hence its slightly raised position on a small mound. Three short rows of new terraced houses lie to the east.

Present-day **GRAFTON ROAD** diverts to the right to join Lamble Street further to the east than before. Continue walking, as it swings past the entrance to **KILN PLACE** on the right. This was built in 1959-62 by Armstrong and MacManus. Kiln Place covers a site used in the 19th century for brick making. Until 1904 the Gospel Oak Brick Works was based here,

built on Midland Railway land previously used to dump spoil from the digging of the Belsize Tunnels (p 77). Much of it had been carried here, in the 1860s, on a temporary light railway laid along Circus Road (later Lamble Street and Rochford Street) to Southampton Road. The railway company failed to dispose of the mountain of spoil that accumulated, despite attempts to sell it when the Thames Embankment was being constructed. When the Midland built a second tunnel, they again constructed a surface railway to carry the excavated clay from the tunnel mouth. There were two fierce editorials in the local paper, entitled "The Destruction of Gospel Oak", with a clutch of equally vitriolic letters. Once again the Vestry did nothing. "Are the parish officers asleep?" It certainly seemed so.

The brickworks site remained an eyesore for many years, and during WWI was used as a massive rubbish tip. In the 1950s the site was proposed as a practice battleground for the Territorial Army. The accumulated debris was finally used up in the post-WWII building, and the original kiln was blown up in 1958. The entrance drive to Kiln Place leads to 4-storey brown brick buildings, built around pleasant grassy areas laid out by the residents, who successfully demanded that a children's playground be made.

Continue to the junction with **LAMBLE STREET**. Look left back along the road towards Lismore Circus. On the north side **No.80**, a garage built by the Co-operative Dairy in 1950 to house its milk floats, was converted to architects' offices by John Winter in 1979. To our right, the brightly painted building on the corner is used by tenants for meetings, a facility provided by Camden Council. The building was a disused electricity sub-station until, in the early 1970s, it became a play centre run on rather eccentric principles. Its director, Joe Benjamin, kept no records of the young people at the centre, so that they "learned to take responsibility for their own actions". Kiln Place residents suffered sleepless nights for years. Opposite, the gardens of **No.1** and **No.21 Oak Village** run alongside the road, but otherwise there are no houses on the north side. A spoil heap stood on this south side until the late 1950s. During WWII a pig farm was set up here and, with the exhortation to "dig for victory", allotments were established on the slope up to the North London Line. Local residents can remember strawberries growing there. When victory came, Oak Village, in common with countless communities throughout the land, celebrated the peace with a street tea party **[30]**.

At the end of the street to your right is a further entrance to Kiln Place, from which a roadway leads up to **MERU CLOSE**. This lies on raised ground at the eastern end of the old brickfield site; seen from Kiln Place below, its modern, pitched-roofed blocks look attractive through bushes and trees. About half of the flats were allocated c.1991 to the Pan-African Housing Co-operative to accommodate African refugees. The Close was curiously named after Mount Meru, an extinct volcano in Tanzania, which at nearly 15,000 ft is Kilimanjaro's 'little sister'.

We however turn left into the eastern arm of **OAK VILLAGE**, passing **Nos.1-7**, the earliest houses in the street, built in 1853-54. The present 'sun-room' extension at No.3 was erected by Steve Rider, the TV commentator, who was

30   Street tea party, Oak Village, celebrating VE-Day in 1945 (photo Christianna Webster)

living in the house in 1985, but when local children made his life a misery he moved on. These houses also suffered badly during the 1975 flood (p 84). At No.5, for example, the flood water broke down the front door and overturned and destroyed a piano. The police put cordons across the road to prevent theft and the Council provided enormous dryers to dry the rooms.

Opposite, note the entrance to **HEMINGWAY CLOSE**. It presumably takes its name, by association with neighbouring Meru Close, from Ernest Hemingway, the American novelist noted for his big-game-hunting safaris in East Africa, and whose works include *The Snows of Kilimanjaro* (1939). If you choose to scale the heights of Hemingway Close, you will be rewarded with an extensive view over the railway lands of Kentish Town. By now, you may wish to avoid such exertion, as we have come full circle. From the Old Oak pub (p 102) you can take a bus home along Mansfield Road or a train from Gospel Oak station across the way.

Route 6
The Mansfield Road estate

Circular walk from Gospel Oak Station
For modern map see back cover

ere we explore the Mansfield Road estate, which forms the St Pancras portion of the Mansfield Conservation Area, the western part being in the former borough of Hampstead. It is contained by Roderick, Savernake and Mansfield Roads and was formerly part of the Manor of Tottenhall. In the survey made in 1761 for Charles Fitzroy (created Baron Southampton in 1780), the land is recorded as being farmed by a Mr Gould. By 1803, it was a "Dairyman's Farm with land attached, the property of Earl Mansfield, known as the Common, and held by Edward Austin" (see **[31]**).

31 'Gospel Oak Common': boys playing by a stream, possibly the 'Fleet Ditch' (brown-ink drawing by E T Parris, 1862)

Our walk begins and ends at **Gospel Oak Station** (served by Silverlink trains). This was opened on 2 January 1860 as 'Kentish Town', and renamed Gospel Oak in 1867, when its original name was transferred to the newly opened station in Prince of Wales Road known now as Kentish Town West (p 39). Both stations were built on the Hampstead Junction Railway (HJR), a curious line sanctioned in 1853 to provide an easier route for freight trains between Camden Town and Willesden Junction to and from the London Docks and the Midlands. Throughout its existence, the company was a protégé of the mighty London and Birmingham. All its meetings were held at Euston Station and the L & B controlled the Board. The HJR possessed no engines or rolling stock, and never ran any trains. Its company secretary (an army officer on half-pay) left abruptly when war was declared in the Crimea, to rejoin his regiment as adjutant. But the line became a great success, for passenger and excursion traffic as well as freight. Another railway reached Gospel Oak in 1888. This was the Tottenham and Hampstead Junction, an offshoot of the Midland, which had been opened to Highgate Road (Upper) in 1868. Over it ran Great Eastern trains to Chingford. This service continued until 1926, with seasonal excursions to Southend until 1939. At first there was no physical link between the two railways, the T & HJR ending at the site of a proposed turntable that was never installed. A junction for goods trains was eventually laid, and opened on 30 January 1916. The timber signal cabin provided to control it lasted until destroyed by arson on 11 March 1985. The junction was removed in 1922, but was reinstated on 11 March 1940 and has been heavily used ever since.

On 5 January 1981 Gospel Oak became the terminus of the passenger service to Barking which had previously run to Kentish Town (Midland). On the main North London Line, trains ran to Broad Street in the City until 1985, after which the eastern terminus became North Woolwich. The Broad Street to Richmond section was electrified in 1916, but today the 25kV overhead system is used west of Camden Road. British Railways rebuilt Gospel Oak Station in 1954, a rare distinction. At the same time they tried to rename it 'Parliament Hill', but there was a public outcry, just as there was ten years later when the Beeching Report proposed total closure of passenger services here. There was massive, well-organised opposition, and the line was saved. Today it is heavily used, with trains every 15 minutes on the main line, and every half hour to Barking.

Leaving the station, observe on the south side of **MANSFIELD ROAD** the latest (2004) addition to the street scene, a single shop with maisonette above, rather reminiscent of a watchtower. The railway arches are at the eastern extremity of Gospel Oak. Mansfield Road was created in 1806 on the line of an ancient footpath between Kentish Town and South End, Hampstead. Use the pedestrian crossing to reach the south side of the road, which by 1870 had been fully built up while the north side remained open pasture. Few of the original buildings remain along the south side. The **Old Oak** first opened its doors in 1856, but was rebuilt in 1958. Its three neighbours are original. The pub was enlarged in 1879 and four enormous gas lamps suspended from ornate ironwork brackets were added. Lighting was an important issue in Gospel Oak. In 1860, landlord Joseph Hetherington presented a modest request to the St Pancras Vestry: "Could you be so kind as to furnish me with three lamp posts, as I am desirous, at my own expense, to have three lights in different parts of this darkened Village. The Gas Company has consented, if you will favour me with the loan of the lamp posts". The Vestry "could not comply with his request". There was no street lighting anywhere in Gospel Oak at the time.

Continue west, noticing **No.7** with its well-stocked window of traditional toys, the collection of Kristin Baybars, whose workshop is here. Cross over the turning into Oak Village (p 84). The most westerly part of the south side of Mansfield Road was the last to be developed: in 1863-66 rather mean terraced houses with paired porches and steps were built here "by Furnell and others". They had fallen into serious decay before they were replaced in 1981, as the last major piece of the Gospel Oak Redevelopment Plan. The architects were G Benson and A Forsyth, whose work can also be seen at Dunboyne Road (p 77). Notice the red-tiled access gallery, and the ingenious, if rather cramped, planning which provides views through the block and the lower utility spaces, as well as roof gardens. These flats turn their back to the busy street, but the detail of the gentle curve presented to the traffic is of interest. At the end of the block, by the site of former Gordon Villas, we reach Heriot Place, now a pedestrian-only entrance to Lismore Circus (p 85).

The rest of the south side of Mansfield Road is taken up by **Waxham**, designed for Camden Council by F G Macmanus & Partners in 1969-72, said to be the longest single block of public housing in Europe. As its enclosed access galleries face away from the street, it can hardly be thought of as a good neighbour. Mature trees in the forecourt soften the effect, but the contrast with the Benson and Forsyth scheme is instructive. It was thought that Waxham was set back to allow Mansfield Road to become a dual carriageway in future, hence its sound-insulated north front; its more welcoming south front overlooks a protected garden. When the later block was built to the pavement edge, local people

32 Rev. Charles Mackeson, vicar of All Hallows

were greatly relieved that this would make road widening unlikely.

Mansfield Road is already a considerable hurdle to be negotiated, a real divider of communities. Elsewhere in London, local street festivals close their roads to traffic once a year, but this is now unthinkable for Mansfield Road. However, there was one joyous occasion when the street was decorated from end to end, and the traffic halted. We shall see later the glorious church of All Hallows that Charles Mackeson and his parishioners built in Savernake Road (p 107), but it was here in Mansfield Road that its predecessor stood. Charles Mackeson, a civil servant [32], began his task in 1878 as

a Lay Evangelist at the Mission Hall in Fleet Road, which still exists. It was an outpost of the Parish of St Saviour, Hampstead. Mackeson, who also compiled the well-known *Guide to the Churches of London*, left the Civil Service to be ordained deacon in 1885 and priest in 1889. He was given the title 'Vicar-Designate of All Hallows, North St Pancras' when the new district was constituted by an Order-in-Council on 18 July 1894. Such was the enthusiasm for his work at the Mission Hall that in 1886 the Church of the Good Shepherd was established in Mansfield Road, on the site of Myrtle and Laburnham [sic] Cottages, opposite Courthope Road. It was a pre-cast iron church and far from beautiful, but it sufficed for 25 years until All Hallows was ready. The great Mansfield Road Day was 23 July 1892, when the Duchess of Teck, the mother of the future Queen Mary, came to lay the cornerstone, travelling by train to Gospel Oak Station and thence to the site in an open carriage. But Charles Mackeson never lived to see his great church completed. He died from overwork in 1899, aged only 47, and was buried from the Church of the Good Shepherd on 4 November. On that day too Mansfield Road was united, this time in sorrow.

After the first part of the church had been completed, the iron church lingered on for a few years as the HQ of the Royal Fusiliers (City of London Regiment) 1st Cadet Battalion. The cleared site was then used as a parking ground for motor coaches until Waxham was started in 1969. That year also saw the end of the remaining cottages and villas, a motley collection of once semi-rural homes with names like Rose Cottage and Holly Lodge, which had been built in the 1850s. No.123, Derby Villas, was the scene of a domestic tragedy on 8 April 1889 when a 'Mr Evans', who had taken apartments there, shot his lady companion and himself. He was later identified by his wife as Captain Hunt, an army officer. He had fathered a child with his victim, a Miss Greene, who had been "on the stage".

At the junction of Mansfield Road and Southampton Road (p 75) stood the Mansfield Hotel (**[33]**, p 105). The first public house on this site was built in 1855 as the Mansfield Tavern. A change in licensee in 1862 saw the name change to the Mansfield Tower and the granting of a music and theatre licence. 1864 brought back the old name, retained until 1891 when a grand rebuilding took place. The new building cost £3,439 plus almost £1,000 for mahogany bar fittings. This palace, with its coffee and club rooms serving luncheons and afternoon teas, deliberately aimed at the tenants of the new estate to the north of Mansfield Road (see below), which was not allowed licensed premises of its own. The Mansfield Hotel was magnificent, but closed its doors in 1968; its destruction to make way for Waxham flats was deplored.

Cross Mansfield Road at the traffic lights and walk a few yards up Agincourt Road to **Heathgate Place**. This was the development in 1989 that prompted the formation of the Mansfield Conservation Area. The present buildings, housing a mixture of commercial and medical users, occupy the half-acre site, part of the Roderick Road estate (see below), that was not used for housing in 1879. The first tenant was the British Gas Engine and Engineering Company, whose 'Albion Works' manufactured gas engines. The rest of the site was initially used as stabling for 10 horses, but it was soon realised that few tenants of the new houses would be in a position to keep horses. In 1883, a second building was let to Reuben Homan for piano-wire manufacture. This typical Gospel Oak activity remained here until 1987, when it was one of the last survivors of the local piano trade. Other occupants of the site included: wheelwrights, joiners, electricians, mineral water manufacturers and makers of permanent-waving equipment. In 1900 this industrial area was transferred from the borough of St Pancras to Hampstead. In 1909, when the street and borough boundaries had at last been agreed, three shops were added where 'Marcos the Hairdresser' now operates. The Turner family ran a chemist's and photographer's shop for many years, and there was usually a greengrocer and a newsagent.

Returning to Mansfield Road we note,

opposite, the isolated offices of Day, Morris at **No.2 Fleet Road**, also originally within St Pancras. It was built in 1860, and for many years contained the Firefly Coffee Rooms.

Turn left at the junction and continue to Roderick Road, where we pause to imagine the scene before 1870, when there were still no buildings on the north side of Mansfield Road. A stream, shown on the 1801 parish map, ran alongside the road, then a footpath. This was probably a ditch to channel away the run-off from the hillside pastures on which cattle grazed. By 1814 this stream had become the main Hampstead branch of the River Fleet, diverted from its natural course and canalised along Mansfield Road.

When the Hampstead Junction Railway opened for traffic on 2 January 1860, it imposed a barrier between the 25 acres of land south of its tracks here and the main Kenwood estate. One field to the north of the tracks was owned by the St Pancras Church Lands Trust, an ancient charity whose purpose was to raise income from its lands to meet the cost of maintaining the new churches being built in the parish. The only option for the Trust was to let its lands on 99-year building leases, and the Trustees therefore sought to exchange their isolated field for land with a road frontage. In 1867 they elected the Earl of Mansfield to be one of their number and started negotiations. In 1871 the Earl

33   The Mansfield Hotel junction in the 1960s:
Mansfield Road (left), Lismore Road (right),
with the trees of Lismore Circus
(photo Michael Ogden)

agreed to exchange the isolated Four Acre Field for a new 3½-acre plot with frontage on Mansfield Road. Thus was created the Mansfield Road Estate, which extends from the present Roderick Road eastwards to Rona Road, all south of the railway line.

The deal was concluded in 1874 "after the grass had been gathered". There were still concerns, in view of failures on the Southampton estate to the south, that the houses to be built would be inferior, and fears that Hampstead would use land along the parish boundary for a cemetery. The most vociferous prophet of doom was Rev. Joseph Gould Medland, vicar of St Martin's church, who "hears that 25 acres of Lord Mansfield's ground are to be built on from Gospel Oak Station to the Vestry boundary, and … fears that inferior class houses will be erected".

Nevertheless, by January 1876, a Mr Haddock was contracted to construct roads and sewers on the Church Lands estate. By April 1877 the first six houses on the north side of Mansfield Road were finished. 30 houses were built in 1878, 12 in 1879, and the whole estate was completed in 1880. The builder was William Turner of Chelsea. His solid 3-storey terraces in stock bricks, Bath stone

ROUTE **6**

105

dressings (now mostly painted white) and slate roofs, York stone paving and decorative ironwork set a new standard for height, density and quality. Lord Mansfield, too, must have been impressed, since he rapidly entered into an agreement with Turner for the development of the remainder of his land eastwards to Gospel Oak station. Although Turner died before the work was completed, the consistency of his design (with minor modifications) was maintained, and it is this quality which was recognised in the neighbourhood's designation as a Conservation Area in 1990.

Turn left up the west (left-hand) side of **RODERICK ROAD**. This was initially named Wyatt Road, after Sir Henry Wyatt, a former Churchwarden and Trustee knighted in 1874, but the Metropolitan Board of Works, the final arbiter of street names, named it Roderick in 1880. The street name is painted by hand high up on the brickwork opposite, as is a prominent sign pointing the way to Parliament Hill Fields. **Nos.33-35** retain a small section of the substantial cast-iron railings that once so added to the character of these streets; those in Roderick Road were the most elaborate. Most of the railings were summarily removed in 1941 "for the war effort" (and never used). Derisory compensation (scrap value by weight) was paid, and the streetscape was permanently damaged. A letter in *The Times* on 15 September 1942 complaining of the

stupidity of the Ministry of Works received the answer "The question of usefulness or weight is not germane to the issue, there is a war on". At **No.47½**, a minimal 'coach house', we reach the northern boundary of the Church Lands estate. The remaining houses to the north were completed in 1883. The terraced houses at **Nos.65-73** have red brick trimmings and terracotta inlay. Here we reach the former boundary with Hampstead; in 1900 the boundary was moved to the centre of the road and the west side became part of Hampstead.

From the outset, William Turner's houses proved to be highly adaptable. Large enough for the most prolific of Victorian families and their servants, they were even more suitable for multiple occupation, usually by separate families on each of the three floors. Records of the early years of Roderick Road show houses well filled with agricultural workers such as cowmen, farriers and bridle makers, who gradually gave way to tram drivers and workers in the many piano trades. In 1881, No.41 was completely full of brickmakers. Nor were the women idle: 'folders of stationery', 'black borderers' and even an 'artist's model' are recorded. Such industry no doubt influenced Charles Booth to comment of the estate "a very superior and carefully managed property occupied by upper working class and lower middle class of the most respectable kind". Booth classified all the streets on the estate as pink,

inhabited by people of "fairly comfortable" means, with good average earnings. He wrote in 1898 that the streets were "alike as two peas in character", except for **SAVERNAKE ROAD**, which we now join, which was a little better.

Although Savernake Road is first mentioned in 1880, it was not completed until 1899. The name Savernake may have a Mansfield family connection, or possibly with the Turner family who came from Wiltshire, where Savernake Forest lies. The houses in Savernake Road, although of the same basic type which was presumably proving popular, are all red-brick-faced, and the early ones, **Nos.13-23** and **Nos.87-97** have first-floor balconies with chaste railings.

One of the reasons for the delay in completing Savernake Road was the need to agree on its alignment as a through route to South End, where house-building was delayed by the continuing existence of the Smallpox Hospital there. When Lisburne Road, the Hampstead street parallel to Roderick Road and to the west of it, was finally built, unflattering comparisons were made, so much so that Lord Mansfield built a dividing wall along the parish boundary to prevent access to the Mansfield estate from the west. Unfortunately, this meant that his own tenants were denied access to South End, and in 1892 the local parishioners, led by Rev. Charles Mackeson, petitioned for the wall to be taken down. After this was done, Lord Mansfield threatened his leaseholders with eviction unless the wall was reinstated, and it was rebuilt. By now the alignment problem had been sorted out, and an offset made in Constantine Road, still clearly visible. The wall was eventually cleared away by applying the Michael Angelo Taylor Act (an early form of compulsory purchase).

Opposite this junction of Roderick and Savernake Roads is a pedestrian bridge over the railway to Hampstead Heath. (Constantine Road, which continues Savernake Road to the left, is out of our area, having always been part of the borough of Hampstead.) The newly-formed London County Council assumed authority for Hampstead Heath in 1889, but there was no direct access from the south until 1895. After years of argument as to who should pay for a bridge, and where it should be built, this point was chosen because it provided the easiest (and least disturbing) route to the Heath for passengers descending from the tram at the stop in Southampton Road. It was also, conveniently for the LCC who footed the bill, the cheapest option. The original iron bridge was peppered by shrapnel in WWII and replaced by the present concrete structure in 1980. Notice the 'spy holes' for train spotters made by contractors at the request of a local resident, and the planting which is maintained, despite frequent vandalism, by local volunteers.

We now turn right along Savernake Road to continue our walk. On the opposite side, note the large houses at **No.18** and **No.24**. These are in an Arts and Crafts style and feature the so-called 'Ipswich window'. Many of the houses in the road have retained their half-tiled porches and some have kept their tiled garden paths complete with coal holes.

On the right the next turning is **SHIRLOCK ROAD**, originally to be called Humbert Road, and completed in 1882. Stop and look along its length. At the corner, **No. 57** is a small recent addition (1998) with a prominent semi-circular bay. Otherwise the houses are similar to those in Roderick Road. In Shirlock Road in 1901, only 3 houses were single-family homes, in contrast to the present tally of 25. The earliest residents included a stagecoach driver, Pullman car conductors and wood carvers. There was a substantial number of clerks, embroiderers and dressmakers. At **No.8** in 1889 the Mansfield Studio was running evening art classes and at **No.23**, Professor Edouard Aldier was offering classes and private lessons in dancing, callisthenics, hygienic and curative exercises. At **No.47** Dorothy Mary Larcher (1882–1952), flower painter, designer, and textile printer, was born, the daughter of a schoolmaster. Active during the 1920s and 1930s, she produced with her partner, the designer and printer (Mabel) Phyllis Barron (1890–1964), innovative hand block-printed

materials that had "a perfect harmony between the fibre, the dye and the block".

Facing us across the road is the west front of **All Hallows Church [34]**, the jewel in the Mansfield crown. This is the masterpiece of James Brooks, the distinguished Victorian architect (1825-1901), who died before its completion. The land for the church, vicarage and church hall had been purchased from the Earl of Mansfield in 1888, at a cost of £1,380, but fundraising took time. The Diocese of London promised a large donation from the sale of the site of the Wren City church of All Hallows the Great, which was demolished to widen Thames Street in 1894, but the amount received fell far short of the promise and the condition that the new church should be called All Hallows, instead of the Good Shepherd, was unpopular. The cornerstone was laid with much pomp in 1892, and the nave consecrated by the first, and only, Bishop of Islington on 23 January 1901. All Hallows officially became a parish on 7 February 1901. The chancel, to a revised design by Giles Gilbert Scott, was completed in 1914. The great four-manual organ, the last to be built and supervised by Dr Arthur Hill, was installed a year later, when the opening recital was given by Dr W G Alcock. More recently, the bells from St Stephen's Church, Hampstead have been recast and installed for chiming at All Hallows. Although the planned stone

vault of the nave was never completed, and Brooks' timber turrets and flèche never adorned the roof, All Hallows, Gospel Oak is a magnificent building, inside and out, a worthy memorial to its time and to those who created it.

The east end of the church faces **COURTHOPE ROAD**. This was begun by Turner in 1883 and completed nine years later. On the opposite corner is the Vicarage. This was designed by Brooks and built 1889-91. It is a distinguished house from more spacious clerical days. In 1891, the Vicar, Rev. Charles Mackeson, was living here with his wife, four sons, two daughters, and three servants who the census-taker suggests were "living in wooden sheds in the garden".

We turn right down Courthope Road, passing the Church Hall which has been used by Hampstead Hill Pre-preparatory School since the conversion of the church undercroft for parish activities. The first 'parish room' on this site was a corrugated iron structure built for £300 by two parishioners in 1889. Note that the houses at the upper end of the road have different windows on the second floor. There are plenty of garden railings here, but none is original. At **No.41** in 1910 lived Charles John Mann, house decorator and Progressive councillor for Maitland Park, a man of strong pro-Labour sentiments, whose family life, like that of so many on the estate, would soon be blighted by the approaching world conflict. The artist John Sutcliffe, who had exhibited at the Royal Academy in the 1850s, died at **No.16** in October 1892. At the end of the road, an arched access under **No.2** led to rear delivery space for the shops in **MANSFIELD ROAD**, which we now rejoin, turning left.

This parade was authorised by the Vestry in 1881, and of the original eleven units most still provide essential services. The off-licence at **No.62** was originally the post office. This later moved to **No.78**, and only closed in 2004 when the long-serving postmaster, Mr Vik and his family, retired. At **No.68**, Ernest Gruen kept a bakery for over thirty years. He was thanked for his efforts in 1915 when a local mob wrecked his shop in retaliation for the sinking of the Lusitania. No.68 was a dairy for 90 years, operated from 1936 to 1971 by the Express Dairy, which parked its milk floats in the yard at the back. The local grocers Walton, Hassell and Port operated from **No.82** until 1979. It was run for a further 25 years as the Mansfield Supermarket by Jay & George Dattani. Early photographs show all the shops sporting heavy canvas awnings and children playing in the street.

We turn left here, into **ESTELLE ROAD**. This was begun by Turner in the early 1880s, and completed by 1893, with the exception of Nos.43-51 at the north end. Just after the corner shop and before the first house, we come to the gated entrance to **Hodes Row**, a pleasant block of three flats built in 2000 in place of the dairy. Mr Turner himself lived at **No.1** for a few years from 1881 when the yard was used for stabling his horses. The houses in Estelle Road have more applied decoration and have retained more of their original ironwork and gateposts than the other streets on the estate. Notice in particular **Nos.2**, **4-6**, **16-18** and **26** on the east side.

From the outset, Estelle Road contained a higher proportion of single-family houses, mainly occupied by teachers and clerks. Later literary figures included James MacGibbon and his family, who lived at **No.22** in the 1970s. In the middle of same decade, the feminist novelist and cultural historian Marina Warner (b.1946) was living at **No.40** with her husband William Shawcross (b.1946), the broadcaster and commentator, and here their son the artist Conrad Shawcross was born in 1977.

On the west side, **Nos.27-41** are in an Arts and Crafts style with terracotta inlay and the prominent so-called 'Ipswich window' we saw in Savernake Road. Christina Foyle (1911–1999) was born at No.35, one of the two daughters and three children of the bookseller William Alfred

Foyle (1885–1963). Upon leaving her Swiss finishing school, she joined the Foyle family firm, which moved into its present purpose-built premises in Charing Cross Road in 1929. One day, working behind the counter, she recommended *The Forsyte Saga* to a customer who turned out to be its author, John Galsworthy, and was inspired to host parties where book lovers might meet their favourite writers in an informal setting. From 1930 she organised no fewer than 664 literary luncheons which, graced by novelists and luminaries and with her own flair for publicity, became a fixture of the London literary scene. When her father died in 1963, Christina Foyle succeeded him as managing director, and ruled her bookshop as an autocrat. She forbade the use of cash registers, computers, and calculators: even in 1990, Foyle's assistants relied on mental arithmetic or pencil and paper to add up bills. Anyone attempting to place an order by telephone would be told to write or visit. Staff had to put up with low pay and poor conditions. Her refusal to discard old stock ensured that the shop accumulated an unrivalled range of titles. No inventory was kept, however, and the arrangement of books on shelves was notoriously idiosyncratic. The famous inefficiencies that eroded Foyle's reputation as 'the world's greatest bookshop' only enhanced her claim to be Britain's best-known bookseller.

In November 1932, William Hannington

ROUTE **6**

was living in the old Foyle home at No.35. A member of the National Unemployed Worker's Movement, he was arrested for a speech to hunger marchers in Trafalgar Square, having declaimed "Let the working class, in uniform and out of uniform, stand together". He was charged with attempting to cause disaffection among the police. Despite protesting at his trial that the charge was trumped up and that the police force was already disaffected, he was sentenced to 3 months' imprisonment.

Beyond here, we may notice some variation in the house types. On 2 August 1944, a German flying bomb landed in Parliament Hill Fields, severely damaging houses in both Savernake and Estelle Roads, and causing minor damage to the church. At the service to induct the new vicar, Fr Bailey, there was no glass in the chancel windows. Here in Estelle Road Nos.43-51 were taken down and the site was redeveloped in 1958.

Walk ahead and pause at the corner with **SAVERNAKE ROAD**. In the 1944 explosion Nos.42-48 on the opposite side to our left were lost and replaced by flats in 1957, while Nos.58-64 were also destroyed, and replaced in 1951. It was from the original No.44 that Mrs Margaret Nevinson, "wife of H W Nevinson, War Correspondent at Ladysmith", wrote to the *Hampstead and Highgate Express* on 4 November 1899 "Sir, I am collecting tobacco, cigars, pipes and sweetmeats

as a present for our soldiers in South Africa, and shall be grateful of the smallest contribution either in money or in kind towards the hampers before November 24th". Her husband nicknamed 'The Grand Duke', was the author of *Fire of Life* and father of the Vorticist painter C R W Nevinson (1889-1946), who became a pioneer Official War Artist in 1916.

Turn right and follow the road as it begins to curve as the railway behind approaches Gospel Oak Station. On the right we pass the top end of **RONA ROAD**. This was originally to be called Avebury Road, after the Turners' home village in Wiltshire. Rona Road was built from 1884 to 1891. Teachers and telephonists were strongly represented among the early residents. Although the south side of Savernake Road was completed, there was no building on the north-east side between the road and the railway. The unfenced area had been a worry for many years. In 1886, for instance, "complaints about youths congregating on Sunday between Mansfield Road and Parliament Hill ....[to be] referred to the police". (At least it was only on Sundays!)

The last houses to be built in **SAVERNAKE ROAD** were Nos.86-114. The first six of these introduce arched windows at second floor level. In 1901 at **No.86** lived Arthur Garlick, "commercial traveller in spices", while earlier houses on

the opposite side of the road at No.7 and **No.17**, were occupied by Miss Wilkin's Victoria High School for Girls (cf. p 53).

There remained the large corner site which had been used for John Russell's Nursery and for allotments since 1878. This was acquired in 1898 by the School Board for London as the site for a new school. Temporary iron classrooms were put on land next to the station, leaving the rest of the area for Mansfield Road School. This would consist of a traditional 3-decker main school, with infants, girls and boys on separate floors, and also a Special school for children with disabilities, which was built along the back of the site. The playground was in the centre, and the imposing main school filled the Mansfield Road frontage. Designed by T J Bailey, it had rather severe Classical pretensions, unlike some of the more jolly creations of the Board (the neighbouring Carlton School for example, p 97). Mansfield Road School opened on 2 September 1901 with 1166 pupils, and was enlarged in 1908. As the pattern of London education progressed, the school became a Central School in 1933 and was confusingly renamed Fleet Central **[35]**. At the outbreak of WWII, this school, like many others in Camden, was evacuated and the buildings became a temporary Fire Station. On the night of 16 November 1940, a landmine from a German bomber scored a direct hit. Four officers were killed, and the buildings mostly demolished. Later in the war, the site was used as a tracking station for flying bombs. On 21 March 1945, a "brave young lady [an Auxiliary Fire Service telephonist] on duty at the post, tracked the flying bomb all the way across London from south to north, its course in a direct line with her post. She knew it was overhead…but stayed put…the beastly thing cut out and blew her and the post to pieces".

It was 1953 before the London County Council built a new school (called **Gospel Oak School** by public choice) with Miss E Bartholomew as headmistress, and that (with additions) is the school that we see today. In the general wartime destruction, Nos.1-11 and No.114 Savernake Road were wrecked, and eleven prefabricated homes erected. In 1985 these were removed to make way for the present Nursery School building. As we walk past the decorative main entrance gates in **MANSFIELD ROAD** you may observe a brick gatepost sadly imprisoned in a later wall. This is the only remaining trace of the original Mansfield Road School. It brings us back to Gospel Oak Station and the end of our exploration.

35 Fleet Central School, Mansfield Road, in 1933

Sources

Books and pamphlets

Aston, Mark. *The cinemas of Camden*. LB of Camden, 1997

Aston, Mark. *Foul deeds & suspicious deaths in Hampstead, Holborn & St Pancras*. Wharncliffe Books, 2005

Barnes, Eric George. *The rise of the Midland Railway, 1844-1874*. Allen & Unwin, 1966

Bebbington, Gillian. *London street names*. Batsford, 1972

Blacker, Ken. *London's buses*, Vol.1. H J Publications, 1977

Briggs, Asa et al. *Marx in London: an illustrated guide*. BBC, 1982

Camden History Society. *The streets of Belsize* (1991); *Streets of Camden Town* (2003); *Streets of Kentish Town* (2005)

Cherry, Bridget & Pevsner, Nikolaus. *London 4: North*. Penguin, 1999 (*The buildings of England*)

Colloms, Marianne & Weindling, Dick. *Camden Town and Kentish Town*. Tempus, 2003 (*Images of London*)

Cox, Nicholas. *St Martin's Church Gospel Oak: an illustrated history*. Church Council, 2003 rev. 2005

Dixon, Tom. *Operation skyscraper*. Churchman, 1988

Fairfield, S. *The streets of London: a dictionary…* Macmillan, 1983

Goslin, Geoff. *The London extension to the Midland Railway, St Pancras to Bedford*. Irwell Press, 1994

Holmes, Malcolm J. *Housing is not enough…* St Pancras Housing Assoc., 1999

Jerome, Jerome K. *My life and times*. John Murray, 1926

Jones, Dave. *Hampstead and Highgate tramways*. Middleton Press, 1995

Lee, Charles E. *St Pancras Church and Parish*. St Pancras PCC, 1955

Lovett, Dennis. *London's own railway: the North London Line 1846-2001*. Irwell Press, 2001

Marshall, Lesley (comp.). *Kentish Town: its past in pictures*. Camden Leisure Services, 1993

Newbery, C Allen (ed.

Woolven, Robin). *Wartime St Pancras*. Camden History Society, 2006

Oakley, E R. *The London County Council Tramways, Vol 2: North London*. London Tramways History Group, 1991

Pevsner, Nikolaus. *London, except the Cities of London and Westminster*. Penguin, 1952 (*The buildings of England*)

Richardson, John. *A history of Camden*. Historical Publications, 1999

Richardson, John. *Kentish Town past*. Historical Publications, 1997

Scholey, K A. *The railways of Camden*. Camden History Society, 2002

Tindall, Gillian. *The fields beneath: the history of one London village*. Temple Smith, 1977

Walford, Edward. *Old and new London, 1872* reprinted as *London recollected*. Alderman Press, 1987

Weinreb, B & Hibbert, C eds. *The London encyclopaedia*. Macmillan, 1992

Whitley, W T. *The Baptists of London, 1612–1928*. Kingsgate Press, 1928

Whyman, Desmond C. *Shoulder of Mutton Field: the retail butchers' trade in Camden*. Meathist, 2005

Williams, Bridget. *The best butter in the world: a history of Sainsbury's*. Ebury Press, 1994

Maps

Thompson 1801/1804 & terrier book; Davies 1834; Greenwood 1834; Britton 1834; parish 1849, 1861 & 1868; Stanford 1862; Cassell 1862; Ordnance Survey 1869 & later; Bacon 1888; Booth's poverty maps 1889–98; Goad insurance plans; LCC bomb damage maps.

Biographical sources

Chambers biographical dictionary
Dictionary of national biography
Who was who

Newspapers

Camden Citizen
Camden Journal
Camden New Journal,

including *2005/6 Directions, a guide to services in and around Camden*
Hampstead & Highgate Express
St Pancras Journal, 1947-1965

Periodicals

Camden History Review:
6 1978, pp 10-11 [Methodists]; **8** 1980, pp 27-8 [block names]; **10** 1982, pp 19-20 and **16** 1989, pp 14-16 [Charles Fitzroy]; **20** 1996, pp 32-35 [All Hallows]; **21** 1997, pp 20-24 [Orphan Working School], pp 33-35 [Church Lands]; **25** 2001, pp 18-23 [Oak Village]; pp 28-31 [dispensaries]; **27** 2003, pp 2-6 [Septimus Buss]
Camden History Society. Newsletters

Other records

Camden & Kentish Town directories
Census returns, 1841–1901
Hawley–Buck Estate: papers and deeds [CLSAC and LMA]
Southampton Estate: papers and deeds [LMA]

LCC/GLC street lists
Post Office London directories (Kelly's)
Registers of Electors, St Pancras and Camden
St Pancras Met. Borough: rate books
St Pancras Vestry: Minutes
St Pancras Vestry: Poor Rate books

Websites

Numerous Internet resources, including:
cindex.camden.gov.uk
www.camdenbus.co.uk
www.nationalarchives.gov.uk
www.oldbaileyonline.org
www.saintsilas.org.uk
Charles Booth Online Archive
Times Digital Archive
Oxford DNB

Archive centres

Camden Local Studies & Archives Centre (including Ambrose Heal Collection)
London Metropolitan Archives
Guildhall Library
National Archives, Kew.

Index